Warman's®

Bean Plush

FIELD GUIDE

edited by Dan Brownell

Edited by D. Brownell
Designed by Wendy Wendt

krause publications
An F+W Publications Company

700 East State Street • Iola, WI 54990-0001
715-445-2214 • 888-457-2873
www.krause.com

Our toll-free number to place an order or obtain a free
catalog is (800) 258-0929

Library of Congress Catalog Number: 2004100730
ISBN: 0-87349-780-5

Printed in the United States of America

Dedication

    This book is dedicated to Julie Stephani, a fellow editor who generously shared her beanie collection and expertise. Julie spent countless hours unpacking and sorting her beanies and carefully arranging them for photo shoots. Without her help, I could not have created this book. Thank you, Julie! May you discover a mint condition Billionaire #1 at a rummage sale, and may your beanie hang tags never be creased.

D. Brownell
Editor

Table of Contents

Ty Beanie Babies

Table of Contents

I would like to extend special thanks to the following people for their help in making this book possible:

Julie Stephani
Joan Gould
Bob Best
Kris Kandler
Sarah Werbelow
Cheryl Kell
Donna Mae Gerds
Toya Lund

General Introduction

Beanie Collectors are Alive and Well

Why publish a beanie field guide in 2003? Didn't beanies die out a couple of years ago? I heard these questions repeatedly while I was gathering the material for this book.

Contrary to popular opinion, beanie collectors aren't extinct; they're still actively pursuing their hobby. True, some have left the field, but many are dedicated collectors who love accumulating the cushy little toys and will continue regardless of popular trends and economic conditions.

Those who have persevered have done so largely because they enjoy what they do, but they may also benefit financially from the shrinking of the collecting pool. When previous collectors dispose of their beanies or allow them to deteriorate in storage, they will likely cause the value of the remaining beanies to grow over time. Some rare beanies fetch hundreds or even thousands of dollars. As more common, but well preserved beanies become increasingly rare, their value could rise significantly too.

The shrinking of the market provides another benefit to those who remain: enthusiasts can complete their collections by buying from those leaving the hobby.

But whether you want to buy or sell beanies, you need to know how much they are worth. So we've researched the market and produced a pocket-sized reference you can carry with you on your beanie hunts. Or you can take it home and review your collection to estimate its value.

Patience is a Virtue

In the beanie market, as in any market, the key to success and satisfaction is patience. If you are still building your collection, consider your purchases a long-term investment.

If you want to sell your beanies, don't rush. Timing is often the key. Demand can fluctuate widely even over a short period of time, greatly affecting the price. A particular beanie that has been getting low prices may suddenly jump in value or vice-versa. And consider selling in sets. A set is worth more when sold as a unit than when individual items are sold separately.

A Note on Beanie Values

The prices in this guide are listed in U.S. dollars and are based on beanies in mint condition. The values were determined by researching electronic and printed price guides and several online auction sites. They were current at the time of publication, but because pricing is somewhat subjective and can change significantly over time, Krause Publishing, Inc. cannot be responsible for the outcome of any sales. The prices are a general guide, not a prediction of the results of any particular transaction. After all, price guides reflect averages prices of many sales, while individual prices can vary greatly because they are affected by a number of factors, including location, season, buyer demand, competition among sellers, and whether the seller is an individual or a business.

Individuals who sell at rummages sales or on Internet auctions often charge far lower prices than manufacturers and retailers. The reason that individuals set lower prices is that they typically sell for different reasons than businesses. Hobbyists usually have very little overhead expense and just want to make a quick, one-time sale, whereas businesses have to pay ongoing overhead costs and must make a substantial profit to survive. Although buyers may find much lower prices on Internet auctions, they take greater risks on the quality and authenticity of the products.

Calculating average prices among retail and individual sellers is difficult, but each must be taken into account to accurately reflect prices. Buyers purchase from both sources, so neither can be disregarded, but often the result is that the average is a figure between extremes. The prices in this book are weighted in favor of Internet auctions rather than retail stores because while individuals can buy through both retail stores and auction sites, they typically can sell only through auction sites. Thus, because Internet auction sites provides greater accessibility to individual collectors, their prices create a more accurate measure of the value of beanies.

Regardless of how sellers market their beanies, the bottom line is that any item is only worth what someone is willing to pay for it at a particular time. That's the basic principle that drives a free-market economy.

Counterfeiting: Buyers Beware!

Whenever a highly profitable product reaches the market, you can be sure of two things. First, counterfeits will begin appearing soon after, and second, the quality of the counterfeits will continue to improve as long as the product is popular. The quality of fakes is certain to improve because counterfeiters are forced to keep one step ahead of increasingly savvy manufacturers, retailers, consumers, and other counterfeiters.

Counterfeiters have a great deal at stake. Those who produce inferior reproductions are less likely to sell their goods and are more likely to be caught. Thus, there's no room in the market for casual, half-hearted criminals. Successful counterfeiters produce copies that can challenge even the experts, so consumers should take precautions to prevent being cheated.

Tips for Recognizing Fakes

1. Watch for online auctions in which sellers appear to be hiding something. A seller may be vague in the description or avoid giving clear answers to questions. Of course, always be sure to check the seller's previous feedback to evaluate the person's reliability. Be especially careful when buying from a new seller. A seller who has not yet accumulated many feedback comments could be a risk. While the person may be honest but inexperienced, the lack of a significant sales record makes it difficult to determine the seller's honesty.

2. Be familiar with the characteristics of the manufacturer's swing tags and tush tags. Often, counterfeit swing tags will have noticeable errors or defects. For example, the tags may be cut or punched crooked or have borders that are uneven. The tags may also have misspelled words, poor grammar, wrong colors or font sizes, or ink that rubs off.

3. Look for poorly made beanies, which may be made in the wrong shade or size, or have distorted or missing features. For example, the beanie's whiskers might be too long or short, in the wrong place, or the wrong color. In addition, the stitching could be uneven or sloppy, or the beanie understuffed compared to the genuine article.

Authentication and Escrow

If you want to buy or sell an expensive beanie, consider having it authenticated by an expert with an escrow service. Authentication will keep a buyer from being cheated and will usually bring the seller a higher price—sometimes as much as 100 percent higher.

After the buyer and seller make a deal, the authenticator acts as an intermediary, accepting payment from the buyer and the beanie from the seller. Once the beanie has been verified as genuine, the authenticator sends the beanie to the buyer and payment to the seller. The authenticator typically charges $10 to $12 for evaluating each beanie and $5 to $6 shipping, for a total of $15 to $18 per item. Because the buyer normally requests the service, the buyer usually bears the expense, although sometimes the buyer and seller split the cost. While this is a significant investment, it may well be worth it for a valuable beanie. Be aware, however, that authenticators give expert opinions, not guarantees.

If you choose to use an authenticator, be sure to hire one with a good reputation and verifiable credentials.

Caring for Your Beanies

To maintain your beanies' value, it's imperative that you protect them as carefully as possible. Follow the guidelines below to keep them in good condition.

1. Safeguard each swing tag by placing a tag protector over it. Tag protectors are clear acrylic sleeves that slide or fold over tags to keep them clean and unbent. This precaution is important because a missing, bent, creased, or dirty swing tag can drastically lower the value of a beanie, decreasing it by as much as 50 percent or more.

2. Display or store beanies in a dry, well ventilated area to protect them from mold and

mildew. If kept in a home with pets or smoke from tobacco, fireplace, or wood burning stove, store beanies in tightly sealed containers, as pet hair and smoke odor can significantly reduce value. Be sure, however, that containers do not contain any moisture. Add dessicant to containers, if necessary.

3. Keep beanies out of direct sunlight to prevent colors from fading.

4. Prevent dust from collecting on beanies, especially on very valuable or light-colored ones. Consider placing them in plastic display cases.

5. If you have a large, valuable collection, photograph it for insurance purposes. Also record the manufacturer, name, and price of each beanie. These records will make filing a claim much easier in case of fire, flood, theft, or other loss. Keep a copy of your photos and inventory in a safe place.

Beanie Mistakes and Variations

Mistakes are beanies with errors that are inadvertently released to the public. They include misprints on tags, wrong tags attached to beanies, and errors in construction of beanies, such as missing limbs or features placed incorrectly.

Variations, on the other hand, are alterations that manufacturers intentionally make to popular beanie styles. Variations most often incorporate changes in color, but they also include revisions in materials and other features.

Tag errors usually raise the value of beanies only slightly because tags can be switched fairly easily with special equipment. Beanies with errors in construction are more valuable then those with errors in tags. Variations are typically the most valuable because they are purposely produced in limited quantities of the most desirable beanies.

Tag Condition Grading Scale

A beanie's hang tag accounts for as much as 50 percent of its value, so it's essential that buyers and sellers use a common grading scale to prevent misunderstanding. The following grades form the accepted standard for describing the condition of a beanie's tag.

Mint: The tag is in perfect condition with no creases, bends, tears, spider veins, scratches, dents, smudges, or price stickers.

Near Mint: The tag is in almost perfect condition. It may have a slight dent or scratch but no crease. Valued at 80 to 90 percent of mint.

Excellent: The tag may have a slight crease or other minor defect. Valued at 70 to 80 percent of mint.

Very Good: The tag may have a significant crease or other defect but is whole. Valued at 60 to 70 percent of mint.

Good: The tag may have several defects, including tears or large creases. Valued at 50 to 60 percent of mint.

Poor: The tag has a number of defects. Valued at less than 50 percent of mint.

Where to Buy and Sell Beanies

Collectors can buy from both traditional stores and online. Each has distinct advantages and disadvantages:

Traditional Stores

Traditional stores are places of business where customers can physically enter and browse, as opposed to Internet stores where shoppers must go online to search for products.

Traditional Authorized Dealer Stores

Advantage: Authorized dealers are probably the most reliable retailers. It's very unlikely you will purchase a counterfeit beanie from an authorized dealer. Also, authorized dealers typically sell only brand new products, and they normally have consistent prices. Furthermore, you can inspect each piece before buying it.

Disadvantage: Authorized dealers usually don't offer the huge discounts that can be found in other places, and they generally carry only the current beanies of a single brand.

Traditional Secondary Stores

Secondary stores are businesses that do not buy from manufacturers or wholesalers.

Advantage: Secondary stores often carry multiple beanie brands, as well as retired and hard-to-find beanies. In addition, you can personally examine beanies before you purchase them.

Disadvantage: Because dealers do not buy merchandise from manufacturers, you run a greater risk of purchasing counterfeit or flawed goods.

The Internet

The Internet is the modern day equivalent of the Old West, where law and order was sporadic at best. Like the Old West, the Internet is expanding faster than law enforcement, so outlaws can rob innocent people and escape unscathed. Always be cautious when purchasing anything online.

Internet Manufacturer Retail Sites

Advantage: Products sold by authorized dealers are virtually certain to be genuine and in pristine condition. Manufacturers guard their reputations zealously. Dealers who do not follow their strict rules risk losing their license to sell the company's products.

Disadvantage: Authorized dealers usually only carry only a single brand because they have exclusive contracts with manufacturers, who don't want their dealers selling competing brands. In addition, authorized dealers usually only sell current beanies.

Internet Secondary Store Sites

Advantage: Secondary stores often offer a wide variety of lines, as well as retired and rare beanies.

Disadvantage: While the best sites are honest and reliable, you may find some that are deceptive or outright dishonest. Unfortunately, if you buy online, you can't see the beanie in person until you've already paid for it (unless you use an escrow service, which is explained on page 14.)

Internet Auctions

Advantage: Auction sites such as eBay, MetaExchange, and iTradeBiz provide access to millions of people throughout the world at very low cost, thus eliminating the middleman. Savvy buyers can often find much lower prices than at retail outlets, and sellers can find buyers for virtually any new or used item.

Disadvantage: Auction sites create the most risk, as individual buyers and sellers may be inexperienced or dishonest. Also, buyers cannot inspect beanies until after they have paid for them. Plus, selling through an auction site takes considerable time and effort to determine appropriate pricing, describe items in detail, photograph them, keep records (including records for income taxes), communicate with potential buyers, answer questions, arrange payment, pack and mail items, and provide feedback. A major drawback of cutting out the middleman is that sellers assume much of the middleman's administrative work.

Rummage Sales

Advantage: Rummage sales may well provide buyers the best opportunities to discover hidden treasures. Casual collectors who have lost interest in their beanies often want to sell them with a minimum amount of time invested. A buyer can benefit when an uninformed seller offers an old, rare beanie far below its real value. Another advantage of the rummage sale is that customers can personally inspect the items before paying and can ask any questions on the spot.

Disadvantage: People who hold rummage sales usually run them as "cash only, all sales final" transactions. Therefore, once you make your purchase, you will have little recourse if you later feel you've been cheated.

Tips for Buying and Selling on eBay

A number of Internet auction sites exist on the Internet. Although eBay is not the only Internet auction site, it is by far the largest. Some of the following tips are general enough to apply to most auction sites, but others apply only to eBay. If you want to buy or sell on eBay but are not already registered, log on to www.ebay.com and follow the instructions to register for free. Caution: Do not use your e-mail address for your user ID, as this allows the general public access your e-mail address and virtually guarantees a flood of junk mail.

The information listed below is not intended to contain all the information you need to know to use eBay. It is simply a basic overview with helpful tips. For complete instructions, consult eBay's online tutorial (www.pages.ebay.com/education/index.html).

Buying on eBay

Searching

You can use either of two methods to search for beanies—the category search or the key word search.

Category Search

Click on "Search" at the top of the page. Then click on the drop-down arrow next to the box labeled "Search in Categories." Click on each of the following categories: Toys and Hobbies; Collectibles, Dolls and Bears; and Everything Else. The first category—Toys and Hobbies should contain the most results because it contains the sub-category Beanbag Plush, Beanie Babies. This is the category in which sellers should list their sales when selling beanies. However, some may list them in one or more of the other categories.

Key Word Search

Click on "Search" at the top of the page, which will bring up four search options. Your cursor will be placed in the "Search Key Word or Item Number" box under the "Basic Search" option. Type key subject words in the search box. Include the brand, (ie. Ty, Coca-Cola, etc.) and the words bean, beanie, bean bag, or bean plush.

Also click on the box labeled "Search Titles and Descriptions." The search normally only checks for key words in the title of the items for sale. By activating this option, the search will look for the key words in the item descriptions as well as in the titles.

If you want to make your search more specific, click on "Advanced Search."

Try entering a few likely misspellings of key words. If the seller misspelled any key terms, fewer buyers will find the item, which will likely keep the price lower—often far lower.

Also try typing singular and plural variations of key words. Or try just the root of the key word, followed by an asterisk (which functions like a wild card). For example, try Harley-Davidson bean*. This will bring up all variations of Harley-Davidson auctions with words such as bean, beanie, beanies, bean bag, bean plush, etc.

Once your search list appears, you may choose to refine your search to make the results more specific or sort the current results according to price. Clicking on "Lowest Price" sorts the list with the lowest prices at the top, which can be a great time saver if your search created several pages of results.

Before Bidding

Before considering whether to bid, read the seller's feedback. If the seller has negative comments, review them so you know previous customers' complaints. If you feel uneasy about the seller, don't bid.

If you have any doubts about the authenticity of a valuable beanie, consider using a recognized beanie authenticator who offers escrow services (See page 14 for more information about authentication and escrow services.)

Also, read the description and payment terms carefully. E-mail any questions and wait for a satisfactory answer before placing any bids. Never agree to pay in cash.

Be aware of the seller's shipping and handling charges. If they're not clear, e-mail to clarify. Some sellers compensate for low prices by charging very high mailing fees.

Ask for insurance if you want it. Insurance costs are the responsibility of the buyer, but if the price of the beanie is substantial, the cost is well worth it. In any case, the seller is not responsible for items lost or damaged in the mail.

Basic Bidding Options

Some eBay auctions offer "Buy-It-Now" prices. You may want to choose this option if you are willing to pay this set price and don't want to take the chance that the final bid price will go higher than the "Buy-It-Now" price.

Another option is to immediately enter the highest bid you are willing to pay and let the auction end without any more participation. You might want to choose this option if you're afraid you might get caught up in the excitement of a bidding war and pay too much, or if the auction will end when you know you will be unavailable to counter other bids.

A third option is to watch the auction carefully and only begin bidding in the last few minutes or seconds of the auction to outbid competitors before they have a chance to respond. This is called sniping and is perfectly legal, but takes skill in timing. You need to aware of how many seconds it takes for your bid to post, and then time your final bid very carefully so your bid becomes the final bid that is accepted before the bidding ends. Depending on the speed of your computer and your Internet service provider, you may need to make your final bid between ten and forty seconds before the auction ends.

You're likely to find the best prices on auctions that end during off-peak times, which are weekend evening hours.

Completing the Purchase

Contact the seller promptly by e-mail or telephone to acknowledge your purchase. Pay promptly according to the terms of the agreement (Paypal, credit card, check, money order, etc.) Paypal is a favored form of payment because it is fast and secure, and does not allow the seller access to your credit card number or other personal account information, so the seller can't withdraw more money than was authorized by the sale. To register for a PayPal account, log in at www.paypal.com, or click on "Services" at the top of any eBay page. Then click on "PayPal," under "Payment" in "General Services."

Examining Your Purchase, Leaving Feedback, and Making a Complaint

When your beanie arrives in the mail, notify the seller that it has arrived and examine it to make sure it matches the description. If it does, provide positive feedback for the seller. If, however, the item does not match the description, contact the seller, explain the discrepancy in detail, suggest a specific solution, and allow the seller the opportunity to rectify the problem.

Be very careful when leaving feedback. Feedback carries great weight. It is, in essence, the primary credit rating for buyers and sellers. Only give a negative feedback if all attempts to reconcile the problem fail. The feedback system is quite effective, and only a small percentage of auctions result in outright cheating or theft.

If the seller clearly has been deceptive and refuses to rectify the situation, refer to the "Dispute Resolution" section on the services page for information about handling transaction conflicts.

Buyer Winning Strategies

1. Look for auctions with misspelled key words, as far fewer buyers will likely have found and be competing for these items.

2. Search for auctions that are ending during off-peak hours.

3. Mark auctions that you want to monitor by making an electronic list. Click "Watch This Item" in the upper right hand corner of an auction page to add it your personal data sheet called "My eBay Page." This will allow you to quickly scan the status of all the auctions you are considering.

4. Make bids in odd-numbered amounts. Rather than rounding off bids, make them a few cents higher. For example, bid $25.07, rather than $25.00. This will give you an inexpensive way to beat competitors who haven't yet learned this simple strategy.

5. Wait and watch. Don't bid early, as this will prompt competitors to be especially diligent in watching the auction.

6. To snipe more efficiently, open a second eBay window. Use the windows alternately to place bids. This will minimize delays while you are waiting for your windows to refresh. A few seconds in delay can mean the difference between winning and losing an auction.

Selling on eBay

Composing the Auction Title

The wording for your auction title is important because the eBay search engine only scans auction titles unless the searcher specifically requests the search engine to review descriptions as well. Be economical with your choice of words and emphasize key words and special qualities. Do not clutter the title with meaningless symbols, words, and phrases such as !!! L@@K HERE !!! Specific, descriptive words are much better at drawing the attention of potential customers.

Creating the Description

Write a detailed description of your beanie. Include all flaws in the beanie (and tags) no matter how minor they seem. The buyer will have a legitimate complaint if you omit information about a beanie's condition. Be sure your payment, shipping, and handling terms are clear.

Auction Options

Length of Auction

Sellers may choose to list their auctions for one, three, five, seven, or ten days.

Types of Auctions

Online Auction

In the most common auction, the seller sets a minimum opening bid and the highest bidder wins the auction.

Fixed Price ("Buy-It-Now")

This option allows a buyer to purchase an item instantly at a predetermined price set by the seller. However, the "Buy-It-Now" option disappears as soon as someone places a bid. Once a bid has been made, the auction reverts to an auction, and bidders must compete for the item. It's not uncommon for a buyer to remove a high "Buy-It-Now" price by placing a low bid in hopes of winning it at a lower price at the end of the auction.

Reserve Price

Sellers can choose to set a minimum bid they will accept. If no bidders reach the minimum bid, the auction ends without the item being sold.

Completing the Sale

Packing and Mailing the Item

As soon as buyer has contacted you and made payment, acknowledge the payment, pack the item carefully, mail it, and notify the customer that the item has been mailed.

Leaving Feedback and Making a Complaint

If payment has been made promptly, leave positive feedback for the buyer. If not, contact the buyer to try to resolve the problem. As a last resort, give negative feedback and refer to the "Dispute Resolution" section of eBay's services page for information about handling transaction conflicts.

Seller Winning Strategies

1. Include a photo. This is critical for two reasons. First, a photo makes your auction much more visible to prospective customers. Second, a photo adds a great deal of credibility to your auction. Providing a good quality photo makes you look more professional and enables a buyer to inspect the beanie before placing a bid.

2. List auctions to run over weekends but end during peak hours on weekday evenings. While a large number of people view auctions at various times over a weekend, more people are available at the same time to compete during weekday evenings.

3. Set ten-day auctions to allow more time for potential customers to spot your auction

and put it on their watch list. Increasing the number of competitors often results in higher final bids.

4. Avoid setting a reserve price. Many buyers won't even consider an auction with a reserve price because they believe it means they have no chance of getting a bargain. To minimize risk while keeping your auction attractive to as wide a range of buyers as possible, skip the reserve price option but begin with the lowest minimum bid you are willing to accept.

5. Advertise any other auctions you may be running and offer to combine shipping, or offer free shipping.

Internet Resources:

The following are Web sites that sell beanies and/or provide information. Krause Publications is not affiliated with, nor does it endorse or guarantee the reliability of any of these sites. They are listed solely as a convenience to the reader.

Internet auction sites:

eBay (www.ebay.com)
MetaExchange (www.metaexchange.com)
iTradeBiz (www.itradebiz.com)

Manufacturer's Web sites

(Information only; sales through retailers):
Coca Cola beanies by Cavanagh
(www.cavanaghgrp.com)
Collecticritters (www.collecticritters.com)
Cooperstown Bears (www.cooperstown
bears.com)
Meanies (www.meanies.com)
Peaceables (www.peaceableplanet.com)
Puffkins (www.swibco.com)

Online Stores (Single beanie brands)

Disney Store (www.disneystore.go.com)
Grateful Dead beanies (www.liquidblue.com)
Ty (www.ty.com)
Warner Bros. (www.wbshop.com)

Online Stores (Multiple beanie brands)

These are just a few of the hundreds of sites on the Internet:

BeanieBiz.com (www.beaniebiz.com)
Beanies4Beka (www.beanies4bekah.com)
Beanies n' Boyd's
(www.beaniesnboyds.com)
Beanietown-USA (www.beanietown
usa.com)
Best Bears.com (www.bestbears.com)
Collector's Paradise (www.collectors
paradise.com)
Cuddly Collectibles (www.cuddly
collectibles.com)
Elyssa's Treasures
(www.elyssastreasures.com)
Frank's Bakery and Cookie Shop
Collectibles (www.hungrybear.com)
I Luv Collectibles (www.iluvcollectibles.com)
Jeans Beans (www.mencik.com/jeanbean)
Kumachans (www.kumachans.com)
Leahland (www.leahland.com)
Planet Beans (www.planetbeans.com)
Sherry's Collectible Treasures (www.col
lectibletreasures.net)

Shopoli.com (www.shopoli.com)
Toni's Collectibles
(www.toniscollectibles.com/storefront)
Turtle Trail (www.theturtletrail.com)
Twins Two.com (www.twinstwo.com)

Online Beanie Information:

AboutBeanies.com (www.about
beanies.com)
Beanieholics (www.randyandtheresa.com)
BeanieMom (www.beaniemom.com)
Beanie Phenomenon (www.beanie
phenomenon.com)
CollectiblezSpot (www.collectiblezspot.net)
Doodle's Page (www.doodlespage.com)
Ms. Janie's Collector's Studio (www.ms
janie.com)
Sal's Attic (www.salsattic.com)
SmartCollecting.com (www.smart
collecting.com)

Ty Bean Plush Introduction

In 1993, H. Ty Warner released the "original nine" Beanie Babies, beginning a craze that took the world by storm. In the following decade, Ty, Inc. produced millions of beanie creations in a myriad of shapes, colors, and sizes, prompting dozens of other manufacturers to follow suit.

While plush toys had been around for years, Ty discovered the secret to marketing them—aiming for the child consumer. The company designed beanies small enough to fit in a pocket and priced them so children could buy them with their allowance money. Another factor in Ty's success is that it limited its distributors, refusing to sell to large chain stores, preferring small gift stores instead. And, at least at first, Ty limited the production of its beanies. In more recent years, in response to public outcry, it has increased the number of each design produced. Of course, this means highly sought after beanies are available to more people, but their greater availability also decreases their value on the secondary market.

The real beanie frenzy began in 1997 when Ty partnered with McDonald's in a national campaign. Customers received a Teenie Beanie Baby with each Happy Meal. The Teenie Beanies were so popular that McDonald's stores ran out of them almost immediately, creating skyrocketing prices on the secondary market, and, in turn, raising the secondary prices of Beanie Babies.

In late 1999, Ty announced it would retire all Beanie Babies, reigniting interest among collectors. After conducting a massive internet survey, however, it decided to continue producing new Beanie Babies. Ty now has more than a dozen lines of beanies and continues as the leader in the plush toy market.

Ty Beanie Baby
Hang Tags and Tush Tags

Each Ty Beanie Baby has two tags—a hang tag and a tush tag. The hang tag is a heart-shaped cardboard tag attached to a beanie with a plastic fastener. The tag is sometimes called a swing tag because it swings loosely from its fastener. The tush tag is a cloth tag bearing manufacturing information that is sewn into a beanie's seam.

A number of hang and tush tag variations, known as generations, have been used. Variations exist within generations and a number of special variations have been made as well. This guide does not cover all versions of tags but focuses on the most widely distributed ones.

A Beanie Baby's value can be dramatically affected by the generation of its tags, especially its hang tags. Two identical beanies in identical condition can vary in value by hundreds of dollars because of the difference of a single generation. Thus, being able to distinguish between tag generations is critical.

The following photos and descriptions will help you identify the most common variations of Beanie Baby hang and tush tags.

The Beanie Babies™ Collection
Humphrey™ -Style 4060
®1993 Ty Inc. Oakbrook, IL USA
All Rights Reseved. Caution
Remove this tag before giving
toy to a child For ages 5 and up
Handmade in China
Surface
Wash

First Generation

The first generation tag is the only one of the eleven that doesn't open like a book. The front of the tag is red with a gold border and "TY" printed on the center in thin white letters. On the back is the beanie's name and style number, copyright and care information, and the country of manufacture.

The Beanie Babies™ Collection

Daisy™ -Style 4006

®1993 Ty Inc. Oakbrook, IL USA
All Rights Reserved. Caution
Remove this tag before giving
toy to a child For ages 5 and up
Handmade in China
Surface
Wash

Daisy™ -Style 4006

to _____

from _____

with
love

Second Generation

The most common second generation tags feature a bar code and the words, "Retain Tag For Reference" on the back. Copyright and care information appear on the left inside section. The right inside section shows the beanie's name, style number, and the words "to, "from," and "with love."

Please remove all swing tags
before giving this item to a child

0 08421 08005 2
Retain Tag For Reference
For ages 3 and up
Surface
Wash

The Beanie Babies™ Collection

© Ty Inc.
Oakbrook IL. U.S.A.

© Ty UK Ltd.
Fareham, Hants
PO15 5TX

© Ty Deutschland
90008 Nürnberg

Handmade in China

Woolly ™ style 8005

to _____

from _____

with

love

Third Generation

The most prevalent third generation tags feature a heart with slightly rounder shape and larger, rounder "TY" letters on the front. On the inside left panel, a trademark symbol appears after "Beanie Babies" in the header. Below the header, three corporate addresses are listed with a copyright symbol before each. Above the bar code on the back is a warning to remove swing tags before giving to a child.

Please remove all swing tags
before giving this item to a child

0 08421 04108 4
Retain Tag For Reference
For ages 3 and up
Surface
Wash

BEANIE
ORIGINAL
BABY

ty

The Beanie Babies™ Collection

© Ty Inc.
Oakbrook IL. U.S.A.

© Ty UK Ltd.
Fareham, Hants
PO15 5TX

© Ty Deutschland
90008 Nürnberg

Handmade in China

Tuffy™ style 4108

DATE OF BIRTH : 10 - 12 - 96

Taking off with a thunderous blast
Tuffy rides his motorcycle fast
The Beanies roll with laughs & squeals
He never took off his training wheels!

Visit our web page!!!

http://www.ty.com

Fourth Generation

Fourth generation tags feature a yellow star on the
front containing the words "ORIGINAL BEANIE
BABY" and a slightly smaller TY logo. Also new to
this tag are the beanie's birth date, a poem, the
words "Visit our web page!!!," and
"http://www.ty.com," all printed on the inside right
page. Because of a temporary legal dispute over
the domain name, on some tags the Web address
was cut off or covered with a sticker.

Fifth Generation

The outside of this tag, bearing the bar code and Ty logo, is virtually the same as that of the fourth generation. But all lettering on the tag now uses the Comic Sans font. On the inside left page, the trademark symbol in the header has been replaced with the registered symbol. On the inside right page, the beanie's birth date is spelled out; the style number and the words "Visit our web page" have been deleted; and the Web address has been shortened to "www.ty.com."

Sixth Generation

On the front of sixth generation tags, a holographic
star marked with "2000" replaces the yellow star.
Four distribution locations are listed on the left
inside page. On the right inside page, the beanie's
name, birth date, and poem are written in smaller
letters. A smaller bar code and a revised safety
warning appears on the back.

SAFETY PRECAUTION
Please remove all tags
and other accessories
before giving to a child.

0 08421 04620

Retain Tag For Reference
Surface
Wash

The Beanie Babies Collection®

© Ty Inc.

© Ty Canada

© Ty Japan

© Ty Europe
Gosport, PO13 OFP

Handmade in China

Celebrations™

50th Anniversary: June 3, 2002

Her Majesty, Queen Elizabeth,
celebrates her Golden Jubilee this year,
making her the fifth-longest reigning
Monarch.

www.ty.com

Seventh Generation

This tag is found on beanies released in the U.K. It displays three significant changes from the sixth generation tags. First, the word "BEANIES," rather than "2000," is written across the star on the front. Second, "Gosport (or Gasport), P013 OFP" appears beneath the "Ty Europe" listing. And third, the wording of the safety warning has been revised.

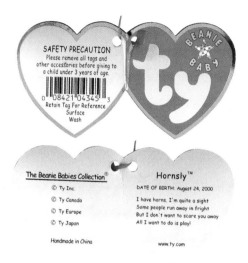

SAFETY PRECAUTION
Please remove all tags and
other accessories before giving to
a child under 3 years of age.

0 08421 04345 3
Retain Tag For Reference
Surface
Wash

The Beanie Babies Collection®

© Ty Inc.

© Ty Canada

© Ty Europe

© Ty Japan

Handmade in China

Hornsly™

DATE OF BIRTH: August 24, 2000

I have horns, I'm quite a sight
Some people run away in fright
But I don't want to scare you away
All I want to do is play!

www.ty.com

Eighth Generation

Eighth generation tags are essentially the same as sixth generation tags, except that on the front, the words, "BEANIE BABY" are written in a circle around the holographic star.

SAFETY PRECAUTION
Please remove all swing tags
and other accessories.

STORE
www.ty.com
Retain Tag For Reference.
For Ages 3 And Up
Surface Wash

100% of Ty's profit
from the original purchase of this
Courage Beanie Baby will be donated to
The New York Police & Fire Widows' &
Children's Benefit Fund.

POLICE DEPARTMENT
CITY OF NEW YORK

www.ty.com

COURAGE™

To honor our heroes
who lost their lives in the
national catastrophe that
took place on September 11, 2001.
We mourn for them and express our
deepest sympathy to their families.

God Bless America

Ninth Generation

These tags are almost identical to eighth genera-
tion tags. The one slight change is that on the front,
"BEANIE BABY" is now plural, so it reads, "BEANIE
BABIES" instead.

SAFETY PRECAUTION
Please remove all swing tags
and other accessories.

0 08421 04531 0

Retain Tag For Reference.
For Ages 3 And Up
Surface Wash

The Beanie Babies Collection®

© Ty Inc.
© Ty Canada
© Ty Europe
© Ty Japan

Handmade in China

Liberty™

DATE OF BIRTH: June 14, 2001

My colors are red, white and blue
It's just not me, they wear them, too
Line us up and you will see
How beautiful the flag can be!

www.ty.com

Tenth Generation

Tenth generation tags feature a significant change
to the front of the tag. The single holographic star is
replaced by five holographic stars above the words,
"BEANIE BABIES," which are printed in a curve
above the "Y" in "TY."

SAFETY PRECAUTION
Please remove all swing tags
and other accessories.

♥ STORE
www.ty.com
Retain Tag For Reference.
For Ages 3 And Up
Surface Wash

10 yrs
BEANIE BABIES
ty

The Beanie Babies Collection®

© Ty Inc.   © Ty Japan
© Ty Canada   © Ty Asia
© Ty Europe   © Ty Australia

White™

DATE OF BIRTH: April 13, 2003

A symbol of the U.S.A.
Americans proudly display
My color stands for all that's pure
The Stars and Stripes will long endure !

www.ty.com

Eleventh Generation

To commemorate the ten-year anniversary of
Beanie Babies, the five holographic stars on the
front of the tag are replaced by a holographic number "10" and a white star with the abbreviation "yrs"
surrounded by a holographic starburst pattern. On
the inside left page, the words "Handmade in
China" are deleted, and six distribution locations
are listed in two columns.

Special Tags:

Certain Beanie Babies have received unique tags. The special editions include e-Beanies, Zodiac beanies, Birthday beanies, Holiday beanies, Jingle Beanies, charity beanies, and exclusive beanies. Most of these tags are variations of the eleven generations noted above.

© 1993 TY INC.,
OAKBROOK IL. U.S.A.
ALL RIGHTS RESERVED
HANDMADE IN CHINA
SURFACE WASHABLE

ALL NEW MATERIAL
POLYESTER FIBER
& P.V.C. PELLETS
PA. REG # 1965
FOR AGES 3 AND UP

First Generation

This looped, black-and-white tag is printed with
either a 1993 or 1995 copyright date and lists the
country of origin as China or Korea. The tag does
not include the beanie's name, and some tags do
not have the CE symbol (Conformite Europeene) or
the words, "FOR AGES 3 AND UP."

Second Generation

This tag features a large red heart with a white Ty logo in the center and a registered mark below and to the right. Like the first generation tag, the tags display the 1993 or 1995 copyright date and a Korean or Chinese origin. Also, the beanie name is not included, and some tags do not carry the "FOR AGES 3 AND UP" statement.

The
Beanie Babies
Collection™

ty®

Garcia

HANDMADE IN CHINA
© 1993 TY INC.,
OAKBROOK IL, U.S.A
SURFACE WASHABLE
ALL NEW MATERIAL
POLYESTER FIBER
& P.V.C PELLETS CE
REG. NO PA. 1965(KR)

Third Generation

The most significant change in this tag is the much
smaller heart size and the inclusion of the beanie's
name at the bottom and the phrase, "The Beanie
Babies Collection" at the top.

Fourth Generation

The first fourth generation tush tags were actually third generation tags that carried a sticker with a small red star placed to the left of the heart. Later fourth generation tags had stars printed directly on the tag.

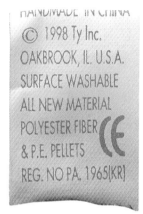

Fifth Generation

This tag displays a registered symbol after the words "Beanie Babies" at the top of the tag. Also, the trademark symbol is added after the beanie name at the bottom of the tag.

Sixth Generation

On sixth generation tags, a single registered symbol in the line "THE BEANIE BABIES COLLECTION," replaces the trademark and registered symbols found in this line in the fifth generation tag. The tags may list either P.E. or P.V.C. pellets as fillings, and some versions feature a red or purple Chinese stamp inside the loop to identify the factory in which the beanie was manufactured.

© 1999 TY INC.,
OAKBROOK, IL. U.S.A.
SURFACE WASHABLE
ALL NEW MATERIAL
POLYESTER FIBER
& P.E. PELLETS
REG.NO PA. 1965(KR)

BEANIE BABIES
Collection®

Germania™

HANDMADE IN CHINA

Seventh Generation

This generation tag features a hologram displaying a heart and the words, "The BEANIE BABIES Collection." The heart is printed with heat-sensitive disappearing ink to make counterfeiting even more difficult. None of the loops contain Chinese stamps.

Eighth Generation

Eighth generation tags are identical to seventh generation tags, except that they are no longer made as loops.

HANDMADE IN CHINA

© 2000 TY INC.,
OAKBROOK, IL. U.S.A.
SURFACE WASHABLE
ALL NEW MATERIAL
POLYESTER FIBER
& P.E. PELLETS
REG.NO PA 1965(KR)

Lefty 2000™

Ninth Generation

The looped tag returned with the ninth generation. Inside the loop is an eight character code comprised of a combination of letters and numbers. Within the hologram, "BEANIE" appears above and "BABIES" below the heart, with alternating "TY" and star images inside the heart. In addition, small stars and hearts surround the central image.

Tenth Generation

In this tag, concentric hearts surround the main heart and "TY" image, while "Beanie Babies" is printed in a repeated diagonal pattern in the background.

HANDMADE IN CHINA

© 2001 TY INC.,
OAKBROOK, IL. U.S.A.
SURFACE WASHABLE
ALL NEW MATERIAL
POLYESTER FIBER
& P.E. PELLETS
REG.NO PA. 1965(KR)

Eleventh Generation

The main image in the eleventh generation hologram is an alternating Beanie Bear and Ty heart logo. The background is filled with various sized hearts and stars.

Twelfth Generation

In the twelfth generation, the Ty heart logo is tilted and off center, and the stars and hearts in the background are smaller. Some tags have a much larger CE symbol on the back.

HANDMADE IN CHINA
© 2003 TY INC.,
OAKBROOK, IL. U.S.A.
SURFACE WASHABLE
ALL NEW MATERIAL
POLYESTER FIBER
& P.E. PELLETS

C E

REG.NO PA. 1965(KR)

Ronnie™

Thirteenth Generation

After creating a series of increasingly complex tush tags, Ty reverted to a simple design resembling its second generation tag. The thirteenth generation, however, uses a shiny red foil heart and retains the beanie's name at the bottom.

Not to be removed until delivered to the consumer
This label is affixed in compliance with the Upholstered and Stuffed Articles Act
This article contains NEW MATERIAL ONLY
Made by Ont. Reg. No. **20B6484**
Content: Plastic Pellets Polyester Fibers
Made in China

Ne pas enlever avant livraison au consommateur
Cette étiquette est apposée conformément à loi sur les articles rembourrés
Cet article contient MATÉRIAU NEUF SEULEMENT
Fabriqué par No d'enrg.Ont. **20B6484**
Contenu: Boulette de plastique Fibres de Polyester
Fabriqué en Chine

Canadian

Beanies sold in Canada have an additional tag to meet Canadian regulations. The tag is printed in both English and French.

Ty Beanie Babies

Ty created the "Original Nine" Beanie Babies in 1993 and began releasing them early in 1994. Although they weren't an immediate success, they caught on after Ty announced the first beanie retirements in 1996. In 1999, Ty announced it would retire all Beanie Babies at the end of the year. When collectors protested, however, Ty reversed its decision. Ty continued producing Beanie Babies and celebrated its tenth anniversary in 2003.

1997 Holiday Teddy Bear

Released: 10/01/97
Retired: 12/31/97

Value by Tag Generation/Variation:

4th **$11-13**

1998 Holiday Teddy Bear

Released: 09/30/98
Retired: 12/31/98

Value by Tag Generation/Variation:

5th **$13-17**

1999 Holiday Teddy Bear

Released: 08/31/99
Retired: 12/23/99

Value by Tag Generation/Variation:

5th **$9-11**

1999 Signature Bear

Released: 01/01/99
Retired: 12/23/99

Value by Tag Generation/Variation:

5th **$4-6**

2000 Holiday Teddy

Released: 09/28/00
Retired: 12/12/00

Value by Tag Generation/Variation:

6th **$7-10**

2000 Signature Bear

Released: 02/13/00
Retired: 05/16/00

Value by Tag Generation/Variation:

6th **$7-9**
7th **$8-10**

2001 Holiday Teddy

Released: 10/01/01
Retired: 12/19/01

Value by Tag Generation/Variation:

7th **$7-10**
9th **$7-9**

2001 Signature Bear

Released: 07/31/01
Retired: 11/19/01

Value by Tag Generation/Variation:

7th **$7-10**
9th **$6-8**

2002 Holiday Teddy

Released: 09/30/02
Retired: 11/08/02

Value by Tag Generation/Variation:

7th **$8-10**
10th **$5-9**

2002 Signature Bear

Released: 09/30/02
Retired: 12/27/02

Value by Tag Generation/Variation:

7th **$6-9**
9th **$5-9**

2003 Holiday Bear

Released: 09/30/03
Retired: 12/26/03

Value by Tag Generation/Variation:

11th **$4-6**

2003 Signature Bear

Released: 06/30/03
Retired: 12/26/03

Value by Tag Generation/Variation:

11th **$4-6**

☮ Bear

Released: 03/19/02
Retired: n/a

Value by Tag Generation/Variation:

11th **$8-11**

Addison

Released: 05/20/01
Retired: 06/21/01

Value by Tag Generation/Variation:

8th **$8-13**

Ally

Released: 06/25/94
Retired: 10/01/97

<u>Value by Tag Generation/Variation:</u>

1st. **$280-300**
2nd **$160-170**
3rd. **$32-36**
4th. **$24-26**

Almond

Released: 05/1/99
Retired: 12/23/99

<u>Value by Tag Generation/Variation:</u>

5th. **$4-6**

Amber

Released: 05/01/99
Retired: 12/23/99

Value by Tag Generation/Variation:

5th **$6-8**

America

Released: 09/13/01
Retired: 03/20/02

Value by Tag Generation/Variation:

7th **$8-10**
9th **$5-8**
10th **$5-8**

Amigo

Released: 07/15/03
Retired: 09/08/03

<u>Value by Tag Generation/Variation:</u>

11th. **$5-7**

Ants

Released: 05/30/98
Retired: 12/31/98

<u>Value by Tag Generation/Variation:</u>

5th. **$4-6**

April

Released: 03/01/02
Retired: 05/24/02

Value by Tag Generation/Variation:

6th. **$5-7**

April 2003

Released: 02/28/03
Retired: 07/29/03

Value by Tag Generation/Variation:

11th. **$4-6**

Ariel

Released: 06/01/00
Retired: 12/31/01

Value by Tag Generation/Variation:

6th. $4-6
7th. $5-7

Aruba

Released: 07/08/00
Retired: 04/11/01

Value by Tag Generation/Variation:

6th. $4-6
7th. $4-6

August

Released: 07/03/01
Retired: 09/14/01

Value by Tag Generation/Variation:

6th. **$5-7**

August 2002

Released: 06/28/02
Retired: 10/29/02

Value by Tag Generation/Variation:

10th **$5-7**

Aurora

Released: 02/13/00
Retired: 05/21/01

Value by Tag Generation/Variation:

6th **$5-7**
7th **$4-6**

Baby Boy

Released: 06/01/02
Retired: 08/08/03

Value by Tag Generation/Variation:

7th **$5-7**
10th **$4-6**

Baby Girl

Released: 06/01/02
Retired: 08/08/03

Value by Tag Generation/Variation:

7th. **$5-7**
10th. **$4-6**

Baldy

Released: 05/11/97
Retired: 05/01/98

Value by Tag Generation/Variation:

4th **$9-11**
5th **$5-7**

Bam

Released: 06/28/02
Retired: 12/27/02

Value by Tag Generation/Variation:

7th. **$5-7**
10th. **$4-6**

Bananas

Released: 07/08/00
Retired: 06/20/01

Value by Tag Generation/Variation:

6th. **$4-6**
7th. **$4-6**

Bandito

Released: 06/28/02
Retired: 02/24/03

Value by Tag Generation/Variation:

7th. **$6-8**
10th. **$4-6**

Bat-e

Released: 10/07/03
Retired: 10/31/03

Value by Tag Generation/Variation:

11th **$5-7**

Batty

Released: 10/01/97
Retired: 03/31/99

Value by Tag Generation/Variation:

4th **$4-6**
5th **$4-6**

B.B. Bear

Released: 07/14/99
Retired: 12/23/99

Value by Tag Generation/Variation:

5th **$5-7**

Beak

Released: 09/30/98
Retired: 12/23/99

Value by Tag Generation/Variation:

5th. **$4-6**

Beani

Released: 10/01/01
Retired: 05/24/02

Value by Tag Generation/Variation:

7th. **$5-7**
9th. **$4-6**
10th. **$4-6**

Bernie

Released: 01/01/97
Retired: 09/22/98

Value by Tag Generation/Variation:

4th **$5-7**
5th **$4-6**

Bessie

Released: 06/03/95
Retired: 10/01/97

Value by Tag Generation/Variation:

3rd **$32-36**
4th **$18-24**

Blackie

Released: 06/25/94
Retired: 09/15/98

Value by Tag Generation/Variation:

1st **$230-250**
2nd **$150-160**
3rd. **$28-32**
4th. **$18-20**
5th. **$7-9**

Blessed

Released: 06/30/03
Retired: n/a

Value by Tag Generation/Variation:

11th **$4-6**

Blizzard

Released: 05/11/97
Retired: 05/01/98

Value by Tag Generation/Variation:

4th **$9-11**
5th **$8-11**

Bloom

Released: 4/30/03
Retired: 06/13/03

Value by Tag Generation/Variation:

11th. **$4-6**

Blue

Released: 07/04/02
Retired: 06/21/03

Value by Tag Generation/Variation:

11th **$4-6**

Bo

Released: 4/30/03
Retired: n/a

Value by Tag Generation/Variation:

11th **$4-6**

Bones

Released: 06/25/94
Retired: 05/01/98

Value by Tag Generation/Variation:

1st **$225-230**
2nd **$130-140**
3rd **$30-40**
4th **$10-13**
5th **$9-12**

Bongo

Released: 08/17/95
Retired: 06/29/96

Value by Tag Generation/Variation:

3rd Brown tail **$55-60**
3rd Tan tail. **$58-62**
4th Brown tail **$12-14**
4th Tan tail **$8-10**
5th Tan tail. **$8-10**

Bonsai

Released: 09/30/02
Retired: 12/27/02

Value by Tag Generation/Variation:

7th. **$5-7**
10th. **$5-7**

Bonzer

Released: 07/31/03
Retired: 10/08/03

Value by Tag Generation/Variation:

11th. **$4-6**

Booties

Released: 06/01/02
Retired: n/a

Value by Tag Generation/Variation:

7th **$5-7**
10th **$5-7**

Bride

Released: 04/30/02
Retired: n/a

Value by Tag Generation/Variation:

7th **$6-8**
10th **$5-7**

Brigitte

Released: 06/23/01
Retired: 12/12/01

Value by Tag Generation/Variation:

7th.	**$9-11**
8th.	**$9-11**
9th.	**$9-11**

Britannia

Released: 12/31/97
Retired: 07/26/99

Value by Tag Generation/Variation:

5th	**$38-42**

Bronty

Released: 06/03/95
Retired: 06/15/96

<u>Value by Tag Generation/Variation:</u>

3rd **$235-250**

Bruno

Released: 12/31/97
Retired: 09/18/98

<u>Value by Tag Generation/Variation:</u>

5th **$5-7**

Bubbles

Released: 06/03/95
Retired: 05/11/97

Value by Tag Generation/Variation:

3rd **$42-46**
4th **$32-36**

Bubbly

Released: 07/01/03
Retired: 11/25/03

Value by Tag Generation/Variation:

11th. **$4-6**

Bucky

Released: 01/07/96
Retired: 12/31/97

Value by Tag Generation/Variation:

3rd **$22-24**
4th **$9-11**

Bushy

Released: 02/13/00
Retired: 06/11/01

Value by Tag Generation/Variation:

6th **$4-6**
7th **$4-6**

Butch

Released: 01/01/99
Retired: 12/23/99

Value by Tag Generation/Variation:

5th. **$4-6**

Buttercream

Released: 02/01/03
Retired: 05/31/03

Value by Tag Generation/Variation:

11th. **$5-7**

Buzzie

Released: 04/01/01
Retired: 12/31/01

Value by Tag Generation/Variation:

7th **$5-7**
8th **$4-6**

Buzzy

Released: 07/08/00
Retired: 03/23/01

Value by Tag Generation/Variation:

6th **$4-6**
7th **$5-7**

CAND-e

Released: 11/27/02
Retired: 12/31/02

Value by Tag Generation/Variation:

10th. **$7-9**

Canyon

Released: 09/30/98
Retired: 08/16/99

Value by Tag Generation/Variation:

5th. **$4-7**

Cappuccino

Released: 03/02/03
Retired: 05/01/03

Value by Tag Generation/Variation:

11th $7-9

Carnation

Released: 12/27/02
Retired: n/a

Value by Tag Generation/Variation:

7th $6-8
11th $5-7

Carrots

Released: 12/27/01
Retired: 04/16/02

Value by Tag Generation/Variation:

7th. **$5-7**
10th. **$5-7**

Cashew

Released: 06/24/00
Retired: 06/12/01

Value by Tag Generation/Variation:

6th. **$5-7**
7th. **$5-7**

Cassie

Released: 02/11/01
Retired: 07/25/01

Value by Tag Generation/Variation:

7th **$4-6**
8th **$7-9**

Caw

Released: 06/03/95
Retired: 06/15/96

Value by Tag Generation/Variation:

3rd **$250-260**

Celebrate

Released: 06/23/01
Retired: 10/11/01

Value by Tag Generation/Variation:

7th. **$7-10**
9th. **$6-9**

Celebrations

Released: 04/16/02
Retired: 08/09/02

Value by Tag Generation/Variation:

7th. **$16-18**
10th. **$16-18**

Champion

Released: 04/04/02
Retired: 06/30/02

Value by Tag Generation/Variation:

32 country variations
7th **$12-16**
10th **$15-17**

Charmer

Released: 10/30/02
Retired: 01/09/03

Value by Tag Generation/Variation:

7th **$5-7**
10th **$4-6**

Cheddar

Released: 04/30/02
Retired: 05/24/02

Value by Tag Generation/Variation:

7th **$5-7**
10th **$4-6**

Cheeks

Released: 05/01/99
Retired: 12/23/99

Value by Tag Generation/Variation:

5th **$4-6**

Cheery

Released: 05/01/01
Retired: 08/31/01

Value by Tag Generation/Variation:

7th **$6-8**
8th **$5-7**

Cheezer

Released: 06/24/00
Retired: 06/12/01

Value by Tag Generation/Variation:

6th **$8-10**
7th **$5-7**

Chickie

Released: 12/27/01
Retired: 04/23/02

<u>Value by Tag Generation/Variation:</u>

7th. **$5-8**
10th. **$4-6**

Chillin'

Released: 09/30/03
Retired: 12/26/03

<u>Value by Tag Generation/Variation:</u>

11th. **$4-6**

Chilly

Released: 06/25/94
Retired: 01/07/96

Value by Tag Generation/Variation:

1st **$890-910**
2nd **$720-735**
3rd **$520-540**

China

Released: 07/08/00
Retired: 04/18/01

Value by Tag Generation/Variation:

6th **$5-7**
7th **$4-6**

Chip

Released: 05/11/97
Retired: 03/31/99

Value by Tag Generation/Variation:

4th. **$4-6**
5th. **$4-6**

Chipper

Released: 08/31/99
Retired: 12/23/99

Value by Tag Generation/Variation:

5th. **$4-6**

Chocolate

Released: 01/08/94
Retired: 12/31/98

Value by Tag Generation/Variation:

1st.	**$265-285**
2nd	**$120-130**
3rd	**$27-29**
4th	**$8-10**
5th.	**$6-8**

Chops

Released: 01/07/96
Retired: 01/01/97

Value by Tag Generation/Variation:

3rd	**$50-53**
4th	**$40-45**

Cinders

Released: 06/24/00
Retired: 05/09/01

Value by Tag Generation/Variation:

6th. **$4-6**
7th. **$4-6**

Classy

Released: 04/30/01
Retired: 09/07/01

Value by Tag Generation/Variation:

8th. **$4-6**

Claude

Released: 05/11/97
Retired: 12/31/98

Value by Tag Generation/Variation:

4th. **$5-7**
5th. **$4-6**

Clover

Released: 12/27/01
Retired: 05/24/02

Value by Tag Generation/Variation:

7th **$7-9**
9th **$5-8**
10th **$5-8**

Clubby

Released: 05/01/98
Retired: 03/15/99

Value by Tag Generation/Variation:

5th **$14-16**

Clubby II

Released: 05/01/99
Retired: 12/23/99

Value by Tag Generation/Variation:

5th. **$10-12**

Clubby III

Released: 09/18/00
Retired: 12/10/00

Value by Tag Generation/Variation:

6th **$15-17**
7th **$22-24**

Clubby IV

Released: 09/24/01
Retired: 01/23/02

Value by Tag Generation/Variation:

9th Pastel **$7-9**
9th Silver **$9-11**
9th Gold **$10-12**

Clubby V

Released: 09/16/02
Retired: 01/02/03

Value by Tag Generation/Variation:

10th **$7-9**

Clubby VI

Released: 10/01/03
Retired: 12/15/03

Value by Tag Generation/Variation:

11th Blue **$4-6**
11th Purple **$4-6**
11th Rainbow. **$9-11**

Color Me Bear

Released: 08/29/02
Retired: 12/27/02

Value by Tag Generation/Variation:

10th Green ribbon. **$4-6**
10th Blue ribbon **$4-6**
10th Orange ribbon. . . . **$4-6**
10th Red ribbon **$4-6**
10th Yellow ribbon. **$4-6**
10th Pink ribbon **$4-6**

Color Me Bunny

Released: 01/15/03
Retired: 07/29/03

Value by Tag Generation/Variation:

11th Yellow ribbon. **$4-6**
11th Blue ribbon **$4-6**
11th Orange ribbon. . . . **$4-6**
11th Purple ribbon **$4-6**
11th Green ribbon. **$4-6**
11th Pink ribbon **$4-6**

Color Me Cat Birthday Kit

Released: 08/28/03
Retired: n/a

Value by Tag Generation/Variation:

11th **$4-6**

Color Me Dog Birthday Kit

Released: 08/28/03
Retired: n/a

Value by Tag Generation/Variation:

11th. **$4-6**

Color Me Unicorn Birthday Kit

Released: 08/28/03
Retired: n/a

Value by Tag Generation/Variation:

11th $4-6

Colosso

Released: 05/29/03
Retired: n/a

Value by Tag Generation/Variation:

11th $4-6

Congo

Released: 06/15/96
Retired: 12/31/98

Value by Tag Generation/Variation:

4th. **$4-6**
5th. **$4-6**

Coral

Released: 06/03/95
Retired: 01/01/97

Value by Tag Generation/Variation:

3rd **$64-66**
4th **$40-42**

Cornbread

Released: 09/29/03
Retired: 12/26/03

Value by Tag Generation/Variation:

11th **$5-7**

Cottonball

Released: 12/27/01
Retired: 04/08/02

Value by Tag Generation/Variation:

7th **$5-7**
10th **$4-6**

Courage

Released: 10/12/01
Retired: 07/25/02

Value by Tag Generation/Variation:

9th. **$5-7**
10th. **$4-6**

Creepers

Released: 09/02/01
Retired: 11/12/01

Value by Tag Generation/Variation:

7th. **$5-7**
9th. **$4-6**

Crunch

Released: 01/01/97
Retired: 09/24/98

Value by Tag Generation/Variation:

4th **$4-6**
5th **$4-6**

Cubbie

Released: 01/08/94
Retired: 12/31/97

Value by Tag Generation/Variation:

1s **$345-355**
2nd **$175-185**
3rd **$28-32**
4th **$10-12**
5th **$8-11**

Cupid

Released: 12/01/01
Retired: 03/18/02

Value by Tag Generation/Variation:

7th **$5-7**
9th **$4-6**
10th **$4-6**

Cure

Released: 10/01/03
Retired: n/a

Value by Tag Generation/Variation:

11th **$4-6**

Curly

Released: 06/15/96
Retired: 12/31/98

Value by Tag Generation/Variation:

4th **$6-8**
5th **$7-9**

DAD-e

Released: 05/17/02
Retired: 05/18/02

Value by Tag Generation/Variation:

10th **$16-18**

DAD-e 2003

Released: 05/12/03
Retired: 05/14/03

Value by Tag Generation/Variation:

11th. **$7-9**

Daisy

Released: 06/25/94
Retired: 09/15/98

Value by Tag Generation/Variation:

1st. **$235-250**
2nd **$125-130**
3rd **$33-35**
4th **$9-11**
5th **$6-8**

Darling

Released: 06/23/01
Retired: 09/10/01

Value by Tag Generation/Variation:

7th $12-14
9th $9-11

Dart

Released: 04/01/01
Retired: 07/25/01

Value by Tag Generation/Variation:

7th $4-6
8th $7-9

Dearest

Released: 04/01/01
Retired: 06/17/01

Value by Tag Generation/Variation:

7th **$6-8**
8th **$6-8**

Decade

Released: 02/16/03
Retired: 05/19/03

Value by Tag Generation/Variation:

11th **$8-10**

December

Released: 11/01/01
Retired: 12/31/01

Value by Tag Generation/Variation:

6th **$5-7**

December 2002

Released: 10/30/02
Retired: 03/27/03

Value by Tag Generation/Variation:

10th **$5-7**

Derby

Released: 06/03/95
Retired: 12/15/97

Value by Tag Generation/Variation:

3rd. **$34-36**
3rd Fine mane . . . **$595-615**
4th **$13-15**
5th White star **$4-6**
5th **$9-11**
5th Fur mane & tail . . . **$4-6**

Diddley

Released: 7/31/01
Retired: 04/08/02

Value by Tag Generation/Variation:

7th **$5-7**
9th **$4-6**
10th **$4-6**

Digger

Released: 06/25/94
Retired: 06/03/95

Value by Tag Generation/Variation:

1st Orange **$425-445**
2nd Orange. **$300-315**
3rd Orange **$295-300**
3rd Red **$40-45**
4th Red **$22-26**

Dinky

Released: 01/01/01
Retired: 12/31/01

Value by Tag Generation/Variation:

7th **$5-7**
8th **$4-6**

Dippy

Released: 01/15/03
Retired: 05/29/03

Value by Tag Generation/Variation:

11th **$4-6**

Dizzy

Released: 05/31/01
Retired: 08/08/01

Value by Tag Generation/Variation:

7th Black ears & spots **$5-7**
7th Blue/purple ears, black
    spots **$22-25**
8th Black tail (Can.) . **$52-56**

Doby

Released: 01/01/97
Retired: 12/31/98

Value by Tag Generation/Variation:

4th **$7-9**
5th **$4-6**

DOG (Zodiac)

Released: 08/19/00
Retired: 06/08/01

Value by Tag Generation/Variation:

6th **$7-9**

Doodle

Released: 05/11/97
Retired: 07/12/97

Value by Tag Generation/Variation:

4th. **$4-6**

Dotty

Released: 05/11/97
Retired: 12/31/98

Value by Tag Generation/Variation:

4th. **$5-7**
5th. **$5-7**

DRAGON (Zodiac)

Released: 08/19/00
Retired: 06/08/01

Value by Tag Generation/Variation:

6th **$9-11**

Dreamer

Released: 01/01/03
Retired: 03/01/03

Value by Tag Generation/Variation:

11h **$14-16**

Dublin

Released: 12/27/02
Retired: 05/29/03

Value by Tag Generation/Variation:

11th **$4-6**

DUCK-e

Released: 03/24/03
Retired: 04/30/03

Value by Tag Generation/Variation:

11th **$9-11**

Early

Released: 05/30/98
Retired: 12/23/99

Value by Tag Generation/Variation:

5th $4-6

Ears

Released: 01/07/96
Retired: 05/01/98

Value by Tag Generation/Variation:

3rd $26-28
4th $14-16
5th $9-11

Echo

Released: 05/11/97
Retired: 05/01/98

Value by Tag Generation/Variation:

4th. **$7-9**
5th. **$6-8**

Eggbert

Released: 01/01/99
Retired: 07/28/99

Value by Tag Generation/Variation:

5th. **$4-6**

Eggs

Released: 01/01/01
Retired: 03/23/01

Value by Tag Generation/Variation:

6th **$5-7**
7th **$9-11**

Eggs II

Released: 12/27/01
Retired: 04/16/02

Value by Tag Generation/Variation:

7th **$5-7**

Eggs III

Released: 01/15/03
Retired: 04/28/03

Value by Tag Generation/Variation:

11th. **$4-6**

Erin

Released: 01/31/98
Retired: 05/21/99

Value by Tag Generation/Variation:

5th. **$5-7**

Eucalyptus

Released: 05/01/99
Retired: 10/27/99

<u>Value by Tag Generation/Variation:</u>

5th $7-9

Ewey

Released: 01/01/99
Retired: 07/19/99

<u>Value by Tag Generation/Variation:</u>

5th $4-6

Fancy

Released: 05/29/03
Retired: n/a

Value by Tag Generation/Variation:

11th **$4-6**

February

Released: 12/28/01
Retired: 04/23/02

Value by Tag Generation/Variation:

6th **$6-8**

February 2003

Released: 12/27/02
Retired: 04/28/03

Value by Tag Generation/Variation:

11th **$5-7**

Fetch

Released: 05/30/98
Retired: 12/31/98

Value by Tag Generation/Variation:

5th **$5-7**

Fetcher

Released: 06/24/00
Retired: 06/12/01

Value by Tag Generation/Variation:

6th **$4-6**
7th **$5-7**

Fidget

Released: 06/30/03
Retired: 09/05/03

Value by Tag Generation/Variation:

11th **$4-6**

Filly

Released: 03/31/03
Retired: n/a

Value by Tag Generation/Variation:

11th $4-6

Fizz

Released: 07/11/03
Retired: 11/25/03

Value by Tag Generation/Variation:

11th $4-6

Flaky

Released: 11/24/02
Retired: 01/09/03

Value by Tag Generation/Variation:

7th. **$6-8**
10th. **$5-7**

Flash

Released: 01/08/94
Retired: 05/11/97

Value by Tag Generation/Variation:

1st. **$350-370**
2nd **$215-225**
3rd **$38-42**
4th **$28-30**

Flashy

Released: 01/01/01
Retired: 03/27/01

Value by Tag Generation/Variation:

7th **$7-9**
8th **$7-9**

Fleece

Released: 01/01/97
Retired: 12/31/98

Value by Tag Generation/Variation:

4th **$5-7**
5th **$4-6**

Fleecie

Released: 02/13/00
Retired: 07/14/00

Value by Tag Generation/Variation:

6th **$4-6**
7th **$5-7**

Flip

Released: 01/07/96
Retired: 10/01/97

Value by Tag Generation/Variation:

3rd **$30-32**
4th **$16-18**

Flitter

Released: 07/14/99
Retired: 12/23/99

<u>Value by Tag Generation/Variation:</u>

5th. $6-8

Float

Released: 02/11/01
Retired: 04/11/01

<u>Value by Tag Generation/Variation:</u>

7th $5-7
8th $4-6

Floppity

Released: 01/01/97
Retired: 05/01/98

Value by Tag Generation/Variation:

4th **$6-8**
5th **$5-7**

Flutter

Released: 06/03/95
Retired: 06/15/96

Value by Tag Generation/Variation:

3rd **$310-325**

Fortune

Released: 05/30/98
Retired: 08/24/99

Value by Tag Generation/Variation:

5th **$5-7**

Fraidy

Released: 09/02/01
Retired: 11/12/01

Value by Tag Generation/Variation:

7th **$7-9**
9th **$7-9**

Frankenteddy

Released: 08/29/02
Retired: 10/24/02

Value by Tag Generation/Variation:

7th $7-9
10th $6-8
10th Signed $15,000

Freckles

Released: 06/15/96
Retired: 12/31/98

Value by Tag Generation/Variation:

4th $5-7
5th $4-6

Fridge

Released: 12/27/02
Retired: n/a

Value by Tag Generation/Variation:

7th $6-8

Frigid

Released: 02/13/00
Retired: 12/16/00

Value by Tag Generation/Variation:

6th $4-6
7th $5-7

Frills

Released: 05/31/01
Retired: 06/18/01

Value by Tag Generation/Variation:

7th **$7-9**
8th **$6-8**

Frisbee

Released: 01/29/02
Retired: 12/27/02

Value by Tag Generation/Variation:

7th **$5-7**
10th **$4-6**

Frisco

Released: 02/28/03
Retired: n/a

Value by Tag Generation/Variation:

11th **$5-7**

Frolic

Released: 03/01/02
Retired: 06/25/02

Value by Tag Generation/Variation:

7th **$7-9**
10th **$4-6**

Frosty

Released: 06/30/03
Retired: n/a

Value by Tag Generation/Variation:

11th. **$4-6**

Fuzz

Released: 01/01/99
Retired: 12/23/99

Value by Tag Generation/Variation:

5th. **$7-10**

Garcia

Released: 01/07/96
Retired: 05/11/97

Value by Tag Generation/Variation:

3rd **$150-160**
4th **$95-105**

Germania

Released: 01/01/99
Retired: 12/23/99

Value by Tag Generation/Variation:

5th **$13-15**

Giganto

Released: 07/31/01
Retired: 06/25/02

Value by Tag Generation/Variation:

7th **$9-11**
9th **$9-11**
10th **$9-11**

GiGi

Released: 05/30/98
Retired: 12/23/99

Value by Tag Generation/Variation:

5th **$4-6**

Gizmo

Released: 06/28/02
Retired: 08/29/02

Value by Tag Generation/Variation:

7th **$5-7**
10th **$4-6**

Glider

Released: 11/27/02
Retired: 03/27/03

Value by Tag Generation/Variation:

7th **$6-8**
10th **$4-6**

Glory

Released: 05/30/98
Retired: 12/31/98

Value by Tag Generation/Variation:

5th **$15-17**

Glow

Released: 02/13/00
Retired: 03/27/01

Value by Tag Generation/Variation:

6th. **$4-6**
7th. **$4-6**

GOAT (Zodiac)

Released: 08/19/00
Retired: 05/17/01

Value by Tag Generation/Variation:

6th **$4-6**

Goatee

Released: 01/01/99
Retired: 12/23/99

Value by Tag Generation/Variation:

5th **$4-6**

Gobbles

Released: 10/01/97
Retired: 03/31/99

Value by Tag Generation/Variation:

4th. **$4-6**
5th. **$4-6**

Goldie

Released: 06/25/94
Retired: 12/31/97

Value by Tag Generation/Variation:

1st. **$280-295**
2nd **$125-130**
3rd **$38-42**
4th. **$20-22**
5th. **$15-17**

Goochy

Released: 01/01/99
Retired: 12/23/99

Value by Tag Generation/Variation:

5th $4-6

Grace

Released: 02/13/00
Retired: 06/11/01

Value by Tag Generation/Variation:

6th $4-6
7th $5-7

Gracie

Released: 01/01/97
Retired: 05/01/98

Value by Tag Generation/Variation:

4th **$5-7**
5th **$4-6**

Groom

Released: 04/30/02
Retired: n/a

Value by Tag Generation/Variation:

7th **$5-7**
10th **$4-6**

Groovy

Released: 08/31/99
Retired: 12/23/99

<u>Value by Tag Generation/Variation:</u>

5th **$4-6**

Grunt

Released: 01/07/96
Retired: 05/11/97

<u>Value by Tag Generation/Variation:</u>

3rd **$55-60**
4th **$48-52**

Hairy

Released: 01/01/01
Retired: 01/26/01

Value by Tag Generation/Variation:

7th. **$7-9**
8th. **$5-7**

Halo

Released: 09/30/98
Retired: 11/19/99

Value by Tag Generation/Variation:

5th. **$7-9**

Halo II

Released: 02/13/00
Retired: 04/06/01

Value by Tag Generation/Variation:

6th **$6-9**
7th **$8-10**

Hamlet

Released: 08/28/03
Retired: 11/25/03

Value by Tag Generation/Variation:

11th **$4-6**

Happy

Released: 06/03/95
Retired: 05/01/98

Value by Tag Generation/Variation:

1st Gray **$500-515**
2nd Gray **$385-395**
3rd Gray **$260-275**
3rd Lavender **$55-60**
4th Lavender **$17-19**
5th Lavender **$14-16**

Harry

Released: 06/28/02
Retired: 11/26/02

Value by Tag Generation/Variation:

7th **$4-6**
10th **$4-6**

Haunt

Released: 09/02/01
Retired: 11/12/01

Value by Tag Generation/Variation:

7th **$5-7**
9th **$4-6**

Herald

Released: 10/30/02
Retired: 12/27/02

Value by Tag Generation/Variation:

7th **$6-9**
10th **$5-7**

Herder

Released: 04/01/02
Retired: 12/27/02

Value by Tag Generation/Variation:

7th **$9-11**
10th **$9-11**

Hero (Dad)

Released: 04/01/01
Retired: 05/09/01

Value by Tag Generation/Variation:

7th **$8-10**
8th **$9-11**

Hero (U. S. Military)

Released: 04/09/03
Retired: n/a

Value by Tag Generation/Variation:

11th **$6-8**

Hippie

Released: 01/01/99
Retired: 07/12/99

Value by Tag Generation/Variation:

5th **$5-7**

Hippity

Released: 01/01/97
Retired: 05/01/98

Value by Tag Generation/Variation:

4th **$5-7**
5th **$4-6**

Hissy

Released: 12/31/97
Retired: 03/31/99

Value by Tag Generation/Variation:

5th **$4-6**

Hodge-Podge

Released: 10/30/02
Retired: 03/27/03

Value by Tag Generation/Variation:

7th **$6-8**
10th **$4-6**

Holmes

Released: 12/02/02
Retired: 02/28/03

Value by Tag Generation/Variation:

10th **$11-13**

Honks

Released: 08/31/99
Retired: 12/23/99

Value by Tag Generation/Variation:

5th **$4-6**

Hoofer

Released: 03/01/02
Retired: 12/27/02

Value by Tag Generation/Variation:

7th **$5-7**
10th **$4-6**

Hoot

Released: 01/07/96
Retired: 10/01/97

Value by Tag Generation/Variation:

3rd $30-32
4th $15-17

Hope

Released: 01/01/99
Retired: 12/23/99

Value by Tag Generation/Variation:

5th $5-7

Hoppity

Released: 01/01/97
Retired: 05/01/98

Value by Tag Generation/Variation:

4th **$5-7**
5th **$4-6**

Hornsly

Released: 02/11/01
Retired: 08/08/01

Value by Tag Generation/Variation:

7th **$4-6**
8th **$4-6**

HORSE (Zodiac)

Released: 08/19/00
Retired: 05/29/01

Value by Tag Generation/Variation:

6th **$4-6**

Howl

Released: 07/08/00
Retired: 04/24/01

Value by Tag Generation/Variation:

6th **$7-9**
7th **$4-6**

Huggy

Released: 07/08/00
Retired: 06/18/01

Value by Tag Generation/Variation:

6th **$5-7**
7th **$5-7**

Humphrey

Released: 06/25/94
Retired: 06/15/95

Value by Tag Generation/Variation:

1st **$560-575**
2nd **$460-470**
3rd **$395-405**

Iggy

Released: 01/01/99
Retired: 03/31/99

<u>Value by Tag Generation/Variation:</u>

5th **$5-7**
5th Without spine. **$5-7**

Inch

Released: 10/15/97
Retired: 05/01/98

<u>Value by Tag Generation/Variation:</u>

3rd Felt antennae . . . **$50-55**
4th Felt antennae . . . **$58-62**
4th Yarn antennae. . . **$12-14**
5th Yarn antennae. **$7-9**

India

Released: 06/24/00
Retired: 06/12/01

Value by Tag Generation/Variation:

6th **$9-11**
7th **$4-6**

Inky

Released: 09/12/94
Retired: 06/03/95

Value by Tag Generation/Variation:

1st Tan **$350-370**
2nd Tan **$320-340**
2nd Tan w/mouth . . **$310-330**
3rd Tan w/mouth . . **$315-325**
3rd Pink **$26-28**
4th Pink **$4-6**
5th Pink **$3-5**

Issy

Released: 03/01/01
Retired: 12/31/01

Value by Tag Generation/Variation:

7th **$90-95**
8th. **$125-135**
9th **$85-90**

Jabber

Released: 05/30/98
Retired: 12/23/99

Value by Tag Generation/Variation:

5th **$4-6**

Jake

Released: 05/30/98
Retired: 12/23/99

Value by Tag Generation/Variation:

5th **$4-6**

January

Released: 12/01/01
Retired: 03/22/02

Value by Tag Generation/Variation:

6th **$5-7**

January 2003

Released: 11/27/02
Retired: 04/28/03

Value by Tag Generation/Variation:

10th **$5-7**

Jester

Released: 04/01/01
Retired: 12/31/01

Value by Tag Generation/Variation:

7th **$5-7**
8th **$4-6**

Jinglepup

Released: 10/01/01
Retired: 12/31/01

Value by Tag Generation/Variation:

7th Gr. hat/tail **$15-18**
9th Gr. hat/white tail . . . **$5-7**
9th Wht. hat/tail **$12-14**
9th Wht. hat/gr. tail **$5-7**

Jolly

Released: 05/11/97
Retired: 05/01/98

Value by Tag Generation/Variation:

4th **$4-6**
5th **$4-6**

July

Released: 07/03/01
Retired: 08/30/01

Value by Tag Generation/Variation:

6th **$5-7**

July 2003

Released: 05/29/03
Retired: 11/25/03

Value by Tag Generation/Variation:

11th **$4-6**

June

Released: 04/01/02
Retired: 05/24/02

Value by Tag Generation/Variation:

6th **$13-15**

June 2003

Released: 04/30/03
Retired: 09/05/03

Value by Tag Generation/Variation:

11th **$11-13**

Kaleidoscope

Released: 01/17/01
Retired: 03/14/01

Value by Tag Generation/Variation:

7th **$5-7**
8th **$9-11**

Kanata

Released: 09/30/02
Retired: 02/04/03

Value by Tag Generation/Variation:

13 variations
10th **$10-12**

Khufu

Released: 07/31/03
Retired: 09/01/03

Value by Tag Generation/Variation:

11th **$4-6**

Kicks

Released: 01/01/99
Retired: 12/23/99

Value by Tag Generation/Variation:

5th **$5-7**

Kippy

Released: 08/28/03
Retired: 09/30/03

Value by Tag Generation/Variation:

11th **$4-6**

Kirby

Released: 10/01/01
Retired: 03/22/02

Value by Tag Generation/Variation:

7th **$6-8**
9th **$4-6**
10th **$4-6**

Kiss-e

Released: 01/15/03
Retired: 02/14/03

Value by Tag Generation/Variation:

11th **$6-8**

Kissme

Released: 12/27/01
Retired: 02/14/02

Value by Tag Generation/Variation:

7th **$6-8**
9th **$5-7**
10th **$5-7**

Kiwi

Released: 06/03/95
Retired: 01/01/97

Value by Tag Generation/Variation:

3rd $68-72
4th $56-58

Knuckles

Released: 04/14/99
Retired: 12/23/99

Value by Tag Generation/Variation:

5th $5-7

Kooky

Released: 05/01/01
Retired: 07/12/01

Value by Tag Generation/Variation:

7th **$8-10**
8th **$8-10**

Kuku

Released: 05/30/98
Retired: 12/23/99

Value by Tag Generation/Variation:

5th **$4-6**

L'Amore

Released: 06/30/03
Retired: 09/05/03

Value by Tag Generation/Variation:

11th. $4-6

Lefty

Released: 06/15/96
Retired: 01/01/97

Value by Tag Generation/Variation:

4th $65-70

Lefty 2000

Released: 06/24/00
Retired: 12/21/00

Value by Tag Generation/Variation:

6th **$5-7**

Legs

Released: 01/08/94
Retired: 10/01/97

Value by Tag Generation/Variation:

1st **$380-390**
2nd **$235-245**
3rd **$28-32**
4th **$10-12**

Libearty

Released: 06/15/96
Retired: 01/01/97

Value by Tag Generation/Variation:

4th $150-160

Lightning

Released: 06/01/02
Retired: 08/08/03

Value by Tag Generation/Variation:

7th $7-9
10th $5-7

Lips

Released: 07/14/99
Retired: 12/23/99

Value by Tag Generation/Variation:

5th **$4-6**

Lizzy

Released: 01/07/96
Retired: 12/31/97

Value by Tag Generation/Variation:

3rd Tie dyed **$270-285**
3rd **$45-47**
4th **$15-17**
5th **$9-11**

Loosy

Released: 09/30/98
Retired: 09/01/99

Value by Tag Generation/Variation:

5th **$4-6**

LUCK-e

Released: 02/17/03
Retired: 03/17/03

Value by Tag Generation/Variation:

11th **$7-9**

Lucky

Released: 02/27/96
Retired: 05/01/98

Value by Tag Generation/Variation:

1st 7 Spots **$250-275**
2nd 7 Spots **$185-200**
3rd 7 Spots. **$72-75**
4th 21 Spots. **$105-115**
4th 11 Spots. **$9-11**
5th 11 Spots. **$8-10**

Luke

Released: 01/01/99
Retired: 12/23/99

Value by Tag Generation/Variation:

5th **$7-9**

Lullaby

Released: 1/15/03
Retired: n/a

Value by Tag Generation/Variation:

11th **$4-6**

Lumberjack

Released: 05/29/03
Retired: n/a

Value by Tag Generation/Variation:

11th **$4-6**

Lurkey

Released: 07/08/00
Retired: 03/14/01

Value by Tag Generation/Variation:

6th **$4-6**
7th **$5-7**

Mac

Released: 01/01/99
Retired: 12/23/99

Value by Tag Generation/Variation:

5th **$4-6**

Magic

Released: 06/03/95
Retired: 12/31/97

Value by Tag Generation/Variation:

3rd **$30-35**
4th **$39-41**

Mandy

Released: 08/28/03
Retired: n/a

Value by Tag Generation/Variation:

11th **$4-6**

Manny

Released: 01/07/96
Retired: 05/11/97

Value by Tag Generation/Variation:

3rd **$55-60**
4th **$48-52**

Maple

Released: 01/01/97
Retired: 07/30/99

Value by Tag Generation/Variation:

4th **$38-40**
5th **$36-38**

March

Released: 01/29/02
Retired: 05/24/02

Value by Tag Generation/Variation:

6th **$5-7**

March 2003

Released: 01/15/03
Retired: 05/29/03

Value by Tag Generation/Variation:

11th **$4-6**

Mattie

Released: 04/01/02
Retired: 09/25/02

Value by Tag Generation/Variation:

7th **$8-11**
10th **$5-7**

May

Released: 04/01/02
Retired: 07/25/02

Value by Tag Generation/Variation:

6th **$5-7**

May 2003

Released: 03/31/03
Retired: 07/29/03

Value by Tag Generation/Variation:

11th **$6-8**

M. C. Beanie

Released: 08/14/01
Retired: 08/15/02

Value by Tag Generation/Variation:

9th Black nose **$28-32**
9th Brown nose. . . **$600-625**
9th Signed **$725-755**

M. C. Beanie II

Released: 08/19/02
Retired: 08/14/03

Value by Tag Generation/Variation:

10th **$28-30**
10th With card. **$55-60**
10th Signed **$660-675**

M. C. Beanie III

Released: 08/18/03
Retired: n/a

Value by Tag Generation/Variation:

11th **$18-22**

Mel

Released: 01/01/97
Retired: 03/31/99

Value by Tag Generation/Variation:

4th **$7-9**
5th **$4-6**

Mellow

Released: 02/11/01
Retired: 05/15/01

Value by Tag Generation/Variation:

7th **$5-7**
8th **$4-6**

Midnight

Released: 05/01/01
Retired: 01/18/02

Value by Tag Generation/Variation:

7th **$9-11**
8th **$9-11**

Millennium

Released: 01/01/99
Retired: 11/12/99

Value by Tag Generation/Variation:

5th **$8-11**

Mistletoe

Released: 10/01/01
Retired: 12/31/01

Value by Tag Generation/Variation:

7th **$5-7**
9th **$4-6**

MOM-e

Released: 04/12/02
Retired: 04/15/02

Value by Tag Generation/Variation:

10th. **$32-34**

MOM·e 2003

Released: 04/14/03
Retired: 04/17/03

<u>Value by Tag Generation/Variation:</u>

11th **$14-16**

MONKEY
(Zodiac)

Released: 08/19/00
Retired: 05/08/01

<u>Value by Tag Generation/Variation:</u>

6th **$5-7**

Mooch

Released: 01/01/99
Retired: 12/23/99

Value by Tag Generation/Variation:

5th **$5-7**

Morrie

Released: 02/13/00
Retired: 02/15/00

Value by Tag Generation/Variation:

6th **$4-6**
7th **$4-6**

Mother

Released: 02/28/03
Retired: 07/29/03

Value by Tag Generation/Variation:

11th **$8-10**

Mr.

Released: 05/31/01
Retired: 10/19/01

Value by Tag Generation/Variation:

7th **$6-8**
8th **$4-6**

Mrs.

Released: 05/31/01
Retired: 10/19/01

Value by Tag Generation/Variation:

7th **$6-8**
8th **$4-6**

Muddy

Released: 05/29/03
Retired: n/a

Value by Tag Generation/Variation:

11th **$4-6**

Mum

Released: 02/20/02
Retired: 06/25/02

Value by Tag Generation/Variation:

7th **$7-9**
10th **$5-7**

Mystic

Released: 06/25/94
Retired: 1995

Value by Tag Generation/Variation:

1st Fine mane. . . . **$340-350**
2nd Fine mane . . . **$240-255**
3rd Fine mane . . . **$130-145**
3rd Tan horn **$43-45**
4th Tan horn **$9-11**
4th Iridescent horn **$5-7**
5th Iridescent horn **$5-7**
5th Fur mane and tail . . **$4-6**

Nana

Released: 1995
Retired: 1995

<u>Value by Tag Generation/Variation:</u>

3rd **$1,250-1,300**

Nanook

Released: 05/11/97
Retired: 03/31/99

<u>Value by Tag Generation/Variation:</u>

4th **$4-6**
5th **$4-6**

Nectar

Released: 05/01/01
Retired: 05/21/01

Value by Tag Generation/Variation:

7th **$38-42**
8th **$32-34**

Neon

Released: 05/01/99
Retired: 12/23/99

Value by Tag Generation/Variation:

5th **$4-6**

Nibbler

Released: 01/01/99
Retired: 07/09/99

Value by Tag Generation/Variation:

5th **$4-6**

Nibblies

Released: 01/15/03
Retired: 07/29/03

Value by Tag Generation/Variation:

11th **$5-7**

Nibbly

Released: 01/01/99
Retired: 07/20/99

Value by Tag Generation/Variation:

5th **$4-6**

Niles

Released: 02/13/00
Retired: 03/14/01

Value by Tag Generation/Variation:

6th **$4-6**
7th **$5-7**

Níp

Released: 03/10/96
Retired: 12/31/97

Value by Tag Generation/Variation:

2nd White face . . . **$265-280**
3rd White face. . . . **$150-165**
3rd All gold **$385-400**
3rd White paws. **$38-42**
4th White paws. **$20-22**
5th White paws **$15-17**

November

Released: 10/01/01
Retired: 12/31/01

Value by Tag Generation/Variation:

6th **$5-7**

November 2002

Released: 09/30/02
Retired: 12/27/02

Value by Tag Generation/Variation:

10th **$5-7**

Nuts

Released: 01/01/97
Retired: 12/31/98

Value by Tag Generation/Variation:

4th **$4-6**
5th **$4-6**

Nutty

Released: 02/28/03
Retired: n/a

Value by Tag Generation/Variation:

11th $4-6

Oats

Released: 07/08/00
Retired: 06/18/01

Value by Tag Generation/Variation:

6th $7-9
7th $4-6

October

Released: 09/03/01
Retired: 12/31/01

Value by Tag Generation/Variation:

6th **$5-7**

October 2002

Released: 8/29/02
Retired: 12/27/02

Value by Tag Generation/Variation:

10th **$5-7**

Orion

Released: 07/31/03
Retired: n/a

Value by Tag Generation/Variation:

11th $4-6

Osito

Released: 05/01/99
Retired: 11/30/99

Value by Tag Generation/Variation:

5th $7-9

OX (Zodiac)

Released: 08/19/00
Retired: 05/08/01

Value by Tag Generation/Variation:

6th **$4-6**

Panama

Released: 03/01/02
Retired: 10/29/02

Value by Tag Generation/Variation:

7th **$7-9**
10th **$4-6**

Pappa

Released: 03/31/03
Retired: 07/29/03

Value by Tag Generation/Variation:

11th $6-8

Patriot

Released: 05/01/01
Retired: 06/20/01

Value by Tag Generation/Variation:

8th Flag on left foot . . $25-29
8th Flag on right foot . $14-16

Patti

Released: 02/28/95
Retired: 05/01/98

Value by Tag Generation/Variation:

1st Magenta	**$395-410**
1st Maroon	**$510-525**
2nd Magenta	**$180-195**
2nd Maroon	**$420-430**
3rd Magenta	**$40-42**
3rd Maroon	**$285-295**
4th Magenta	**$9-11**
5th Magenta	**$8-10**

Paul

Released: 05/01/99
Retired: 12/23/99

Value by Tag Generation/Variation:

5th	**$4-6**

Peace

Released: 05/11/97
Retired: 07/14/99

Value by Tag Generation/Variation:

4th **$9-11**
5th **$7-10**
5th Pastel. **$20-25**

Peanut

Released: 10/02/95
Retired: 05/01/98

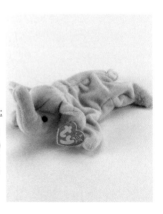

Value by Tag Generation/Variation:

3rd Light blue **$85-95**
3rd Royal blue . **$1,015-1,050**
4th Light blue **$9-11**
5th Light blue **$6-8**

Pecan

Released: 05/01/99
Retired: 12/23/99

Value by Tag Generation/Variation:

5th **$4-6**

Peekaboo

Released: 06/24/00
Retired: 04/18/01

Value by Tag Generation/Variation:

6th **$5-7**
7th **$4-6**

Pegasus

Released: 07/30/02
Retired: 04/28/03

Value by Tag Generation/Variation:

7th **$7-9**
10th **$5-8**

Peking

Released: 06/25/94
Retired: 01/07/96

Value by Tag Generation/Variation:

1st **$1,025-1,050**
2nd. **$575-590**
3rd **$520-535**

Pellet

Released: 07/08/00
Retired: 06/20/01

Value by Tag Generation/Variation:

6th **$8-11**
7th **$5-7**

Periwinkle

Released: 11/28/00
Retired: 12/08/00

Value by Tag Generation/Variation:

6th **$6-8**

Pierre

Released: 08/12/01
Retired: 04/01/02

Value by Tag Generation/Variation:

9th **$14-16**

PIG (Zodiac)

Released: 08/19/00
Retired: 05/11/01

Value by Tag Generation/Variation:

6th **$4-7**

Pinchers

Released: 01/08/94
Retired: 05/01/98

Value by Tag Generation/Variation:

1st	$350-365
2nd	$155-165
3rd	$43-45
4th	$20-22
5th	$7-9

Pinky

Released: 06/03/95
Retired: 12/31/98

Value by Tag Generation/Variation:

3rd	$38-42
4th	$8-10
5th	$6-8

Poofie

Released: 12/01/01
Retired: 08/29/02

Value by Tag Generation/Variation:

7th **$5-7**
9th **$4-6**
10th **$4-6**

Poopsie

Released: 07/31/01
Retired: 04/08/02

Value by Tag Generation/Variation:

7th **$6-8**
9th **$4-6**
10th **$4-6**

Popcorn

Released: 09/30/03
Retired: 11/01/03

Value by Tag Generation/Variation:

11th **$6-8**

Pops

Released: 04/01/02
Retired: 07/17/02

Value by Tag Generation/Variation:

10th **$5-7**

Poseidon

Released: 05/01/01
Retired: 07/25/01

<u>Value by Tag Generation/Variation:</u>

7th **$5-7**
8th **$4-6**

Pouch

Released: 01/01/97
Retired: 03/31/99

<u>Value by Tag Generation/Variation:</u>

4th **$4-6**
5th **$4-6**

Pounce

Released: 12/31/97
Retired: 03/31/99

<u>Value by Tag Generation/Variation:</u>

5th **$4-6**

Pounds

Released: 04/30/02
Retired: 09/25/02

<u>Value by Tag Generation/Variation:</u>

7th **$5-7**
10th **$4-6**

Prance

Released: 12/31/97
Retired: 03/31/99

Value by Tag Generation/Variation:

5th $4-6

Prickles

Released: 01/01/99
Retired: 12/23/99

Value by Tag Generation/Variation:

5th $4-6

Prince

Released: 07/08/00
Retired: 06/20/01

Value by Tag Generation/Variation:

6th **$4-6**
7th **$5-7**

Princess

Released: 10/29/97
Retired: 04/13/99

Value by Tag Generation/Variation:

5th **$10-12**

Propeller

Released: 05/31/01
Retired: 07/12/01

Value by Tag Generation/Variation:

7th **$4-6**
8th **$4-6**

Puffer

Released: 12/31/97
Retired: 09/18/98

Value by Tag Generation/Variation:

5th **$4-6**

Pugsly

Released: 05/11/97
Retired: 03/31/99

Value by Tag Generation/Variation:

4th **$5-7**
5th **$4-6**

Pumkin'

Released: 09/30/98
Retired: 12/31/98

Value by Tag Generation/Variation:

5th **$7-9**

PUNXSUTAWN-e Phil

Released: 01/06/03
Retired: 02/11/03

<u>Value by Tag Generation/Variation:</u>

11th **$100-105**

Purr

Released: 02/11/01
Retired: 06/18/01

<u>Value by Tag Generation/Variation:</u>

7th **$4-6**
8th **$4-6**

Quackers

Released: 01/07/95
Retired: 05/01/98

Value by Tag Generation/Variation:

1st Wingless	**$465-480**
2nd Wings	**$195-205**
2nd Winglesss	**$725-740**
3rd Wings	**$45-50**
4th Wings	**$13-15**
5th Wings	**$10-12**

Quivers

Released: 07/31//03
Retired: 10/31/03

Value by Tag Generation/Variation:

11th	**$4-6**

RABBIT (Zodiac)

Released: 08/19/00
Retired: 05/24/01

Value by Tag Generation/Variation:

6th $4-7

Radar

Released: 09/01/95
Retired: 05/11/97

Value by Tag Generation/Variation:

3rd $60-65
4th $43-45

Rainbow

Released: 01/01/99
Retired: 03/31/99

Value by Tag Generation/Variation:

5th No tongue. **$4-6**
5th Spikes and tongue . **$4-6**
5th Pastel. **$6-9**
5th Hood **$4-6**

RAT (Zodiac)

Released: 08/19/00
Retired: 05/29/01

Value by Tag Generation/Variation:

6th **$4-7**

Red

Released: 04/30/03
Retired: 06/09/03

Value by Tag Generation/Variation:

11th **$9-11**

Red, White, & Blue

Released: 04/30/03
Retired: 06/09/03

Value by Tag Generation/Variation:

11th **$4-6**

Regal

Released: 05/01/01
Retired: 10/08/01

Value by Tag Generation/Variation:

7th **$9-11**
8th **$4-6**

Rescue

Released: 10/12/01
Retired: 07/25/02

Value by Tag Generation/Variation:

9th **$5-7**
9th Left flag. **$4-6**
10th **$4-6**
10th Left flag. **$4-6**

Rex

Released: 06/03/95
Retired: 06/15/96

<u>Value by Tag Generation/Variation:</u>

3rd **$305-320**

Righty

Released: 06/15/96
Retired: 01/01/97

<u>Value by Tag Generation/Variation:</u>

4th **$55-60**

Righty 2000

Released: 06/24/00
Retired: 12/21/00

Value by Tag Generation/Variation:

6th **$9-11**

Ringo

Released: 01/07/96
Retired: 09/16/98

Value by Tag Generation/Variation:

3rd **$18-21**
4th **$16-18**
5th **$9-11**

Roam

Released: 09/30/98
Retired: 12/23/99

Value by Tag Generation/Variation:

5th $4-6

Roary

Released: 05/11/97
Retired: 12/31/98

Value by Tag Generation/Variation:

4th $5-7
5th $4-6

Rocket

Released: 05/30/98
Retired: 12/23/99

Value by Tag Generation/Variation:

5th **$4-6**

Romance

Released: 12/27/01
Retired: 02/14/02

Value by Tag Generation/Variation:

7th **$6-8**
9th **$4-6**
10th **$4-6**

Ronnie

Released: 07/07/03
Retired: n/a

Value by Tag Generation/Variation:

11th **$4-6**

ROOSTER (Zodiac)

Released: 08/19/00
Retired: 05/11/01

Value by Tag Generation/Variation:

6th **$4-6**

Rover

Released: 06/15/96
Retired: 05/01/98

Value by Tag Generation/Variation:

4th **$11-13**
5th **$9-11**

Roxie

Released: 9/28/00
Retired: 12/12/00

Value by Tag Generation/Variation:

6th Red nose **$6-8**
6th Black nose **$4-6**
7th Red nose **$7-9**
7th Black nose **$6-8**

Rudy

Released: 09/30/03
Retired: 12/26/03

Value by Tag Generation/Variation:

11th **$4-6**

Rufus

Released: 02/13/00
Retired: 06/11/01

Value by Tag Generation/Variation:

6th **$5-7**
7th **$5-7**

Rumba

Released: 06/30/03
Retired: n/a

Value by Tag Generation/Variation:

11th **$4-6**

Runner

Released: 06/24/00
Retired: 04/11/01

Value by Tag Generation/Variation:

6th **$10-12**
7th **$5-7**

Rusty

Released: 08/29/02
Retired: 02/24/03

Value by Tag Generation/Variation:

7th **$5-7**
10th **$4-6**

Sammy

Released: 01/01/99
Retired: 12/23/99

Value by Tag Generation/Variation:

5th **$4-6**

Sampson

Released: 06/28/02
Retired: 09/05/03

Value by Tag Generation/Variation:

7th **$6-8**
10th **$5-7**

Santa

Released: 09/30/98
Retired: 12/31/98

Value by Tag Generation/Variation:

5th **$8-11**

Sarge

Released: 02/13/00
Retired: 04/04/01

Value by Tag Generation/Variation:

6th $4-6
7th $4-6

Scaly

Released: 08/31/99
Retired: 12/23/99

Value by Tag Generation/Variation:

5th $4-6

SCARED-e

Released: 10/02/02
Retired: 10/31/02

Value by Tag Generation/Variation:

10th **$8-11**
10th Signed. **$950-1000**

Scary

Released: 09/02/01
Retired: 11/12/01

Value by Tag Generation/Variation:

7th **$5-7**
9th **$4-6**

Scat

Released: 01/01/99
Retired: 12/23/99

Value by Tag Generation/Variation:

5th **$4-6**

Schnitzel

Released: 12/27/02
Retired: n/a

Value by Tag Generation/Variation:

7th **$4-6**

Schweetheart

Released: 05/01/99
Retired: 12/23/99

Value by Tag Generation/Variation:

5th **$5-7**

Scoop

Released: 06/15/96
Retired: 12/31/98

Value by Tag Generation/Variation:

4th **$5-7**
5th **$4-6**

Scorch

Released: 09/30/98
Retired: 12/23/99

Value by Tag Generation/Variation:

5th $4-7

Scottie

Released: 06/15/96
Retired: 05/01/98

Value by Tag Generation/Variation:

4th $8-10
5th $6-8

Scurry

Released: 02/13/00
Retired: 12/15/00

Value by Tag Generation/Variation:

6th **$4-6**
7th **$4-6**

Seadog

Released: 09/30/02
Retired: n/a

Value by Tag Generation/Variation:

7th **$5-8**
10th **$4-8**

Seamore

Released: 06/25/94
Retired: 10/01/97

Value by Tag Generation/Variation:

1st	**$405-425**
2nd	**$305-320**
3rd	**$60-65**
4th	**$38-42**

Seaweed

Released: 01/07/96
Retired: 09/19/98

Value by Tag Generation/Variation:

3rd	**$45-50**
4th	**$14-16**
5th	**$10-12**

September

Released: 07/03/01
Retired: 12/31/01

Value by Tag Generation/Variation:

6th **$5-7**

September 2002

Released: 7/30/02
Retired: 11/26/02

Value by Tag Generation/Variation:

10th **$5-7**

Sequoia

Released: 01/29/02
Retired: 10/29/02

Value by Tag Generation/Variation:

7th $6-8
10th $4-6

Serenity

Released: 06/01/02
Retired: 06/11/02

Value by Tag Generation/Variation:

10th $6-8

Shamrock

Released: 01/01/01
Retired: 03/06/01

Value by Tag Generation/Variation:

7th **$7-9**
8th **$6-8**

Sheets

Released: 08/31/99
Retired: 12/23/99

Value by Tag Generation/Variation:

5th **$4-6**

Sherbet

Released: 07/30/02
Retired: 09/10/02

<u>Value by Tag Generation/Variation:</u>

7th Green **$9-11**
7th Pink. **$7-9**
7th Yellow. **$8-10**
10th Green **$4-6**
10th Pink. **$5-7**
10th Yellow **$5-7**

Sherwood

Released: 08/28/03
Retired: n/a

<u>Value by Tag Generation/Variation:</u>

11th **$4-6**

Siam

Released: 07/03/01
Retired: 12/12/01

Value by Tag Generation/Variation:

7th **$7-9**
9th **$4-6**

Side-Kick

Released: 04/30/02
Retired: n/a

Value by Tag Generation/Variation:

7th **$6-8**
10th **$4-6**

Silver

Released: 05/01/99
Retired: 12/23/99

Value by Tag Generation/Variation:

5th **$5-7**

Sizzle

Released: 12/01/01
Retired: 03/18/02

Value by Tag Generation/Variation:

7th **$6-8**
9th **$5-7**
10th **$5-7**

Slayer

Released: 07/08/00
Retired: 04/04/01

Value by Tag Generation/Variation:

6th **$4-6**
7h. **$4-6**

Sledge

Released: 06/01/02
Retired: 10/29/02

Value by Tag Generation/Variation:

7th **$5-7**
10th **$4-6**

Slippery

Released: 01/01/99
Retired: 12/23/99

Value by Tag Generation/Variation:

5th $4-6

Slither

Released: 06/25/94
Retired: 06/15/95

Value by Tag Generation/Variation:

1st **$1,205-1,220**
2nd. **$380-395**
3rd **$675-700**

Slowpoke

Released: 08/31/99
Retired: 12/23/99

Value by Tag Generation/Variation:

5th **$4-6**

Sly

Released: 06/15/96
Retired: 08/06/96

Value by Tag Generation/Variation:

4th Brown belly **$52-54**
4th White belly **$13-15**
5th White belly **$9-11**

Smart

Released: 04/01/01
Retired: 05/30/01

Value by Tag Generation/Variation:

7th **$5-7**
8th **$4-6**

Smarter

Released: 04/01/02
Retired: 08/29/02

Value by Tag Generation/Variation:

7th **$7-9**

Smartest

Released: 03/31/03
Retired: 07/29/03

Value by Tag Generation/Variation:

11th **$4-6**

Smitten

Released: 12/27/02
Retired: 05/29/03

Value by Tag Generation/Variation:

7th Black nose **$6-8**
7th Pink nose **$11-13**
11th Black nose **$5-7**
11th Pink nose **$9-11**

Smooch

Released: 01/01/01
Retired: 02/14/01

Value by Tag Generation/Variation:

7th **$17-19**
8th **$18-20**

Smoochy

Released: 12/31/97
Retired: 03/31/99

Value by Tag Generation/Variation:

5th **$4-6**

SNAKE (Zodiac)

Released: 08/19/00
Retired: 05/17/01

Value by Tag Generation/Variation:

6th **$5-7**

Sneaky

Released: 02/13/00
Retired: 04/04/01

Value by Tag Generation/Variation:

5th **$5-7**
6th **$4-6**

Sniffer

Released: 06/24/00
Retired: 04/24/01

Value by Tag Generation/Variation:

6th **$5-7**
7th **$5-7**

Snip

Released: 01/01/97
Retired: 12/31/98

Value by Tag Generation/Variation:

4th **$4-6**
5th **$4-6**

Snocap

Released: 11/27/02
Retired: n/a

Value by Tag Generation/Variation:

7th **$6-8**
10th **$5-7**

Snort

Released: 01/01/97
Retired: 09/15/98

Value by Tag Generation/Variation:

4th **$7-9**
5th **$6-8**

Snowball

Released: 10/01/97
Retired: 12/31/97

Value by Tag Generation/Variation:

4th **$7-9**

Snowdrift

Released: 09/30/03
Retired: 12/26/03

Value by Tag Generation/Variation:

11th **$4-6**

Snowgirl

Released: 09/28/00
Retired: 12/12/00

Value by Tag Generation/Variation:

6th **$6-8**
7th **$7-9**

Soar

Released: 06/10/02
Retired: 06/15/02

Value by Tag Generation/Variation:

10th **$9-11**

Spangle

Released: 04/24/99
Retired: 12/23/99

Value by Tag Generation/Variation:

5th Blue **$13-15**
5th Pink **$7-9**
5th White **$8-11**

Sparkles

Released: 11/08/02
Retired: 01/30/03

Value by Tag Generation/Variation:

10th **$12-14**

Sparky

Released: 06/15/96
Retired: 05/11/97

Value by Tag Generation/Variation:

4th. **$35-37**

Speckles

Released: 06/29/00
Retired: 01/02/02

Value by Tag Generation/Variation:

6th **$8-11**

Speedy

Released: 06/25/94
Retired: 10/01/97

Value by Tag Generation/Variation:

1st **$335-350**
2nd **$170-185**
3rd **$24-26**
4th **$13-15**

Spike

Released: 06/15/96
Retired: 12/31/98

Value by Tag Generation/Variation:

4th **$4-6**
5th **$4-6**

Spinner

Released: 10/01/97
Retired: 09/19/98

Value by Tag Generation/Variation:

4th $4-6
5th $4-6

Splash

Released: 01/08/94
Retired: 05/11/97

Value by Tag Generation/Variation:

1st $190-200
2nd. $165-175
3rd $45-50
4th $32-34

Spooky

Released: 09/01/95
Retired: 12/31/97

<u>Value by Tag Generation/Variation:</u>

3rd **$45-47**
4th **$18-20**

Sport

Released: 03/31/03
Retired: n/a

<u>Value by Tag Generation/Variation:</u>

11th **$4-6**

Spot

Released: 04/13/94
Retired: 10/01/97

Value by Tag Generation/Variation:

1st No spot . . . **$1,250-1,285**
2nd No spot. . . **$1,135-1,155**
2nd Spot **$235-245**
3rd Spot **$60-65**
4th Spot **$13-15**

Spring

Released: 12/27/01
Retired: 04/16/02

Value by Tag Generation/Variation:

7th **$5-7**
10th **$4-6**

Springy

Released: 02/13/00
Retired: 07/14/00

Value by Tag Generation/Variation:

6th **$4-6**
7th **$4-6**

Spunky

Released: 12/31/97
Retired: 03/31/99

Value by Tag Generation/Variation:

5th **$5-7**

Squealer

Released: 01/08/94
Retired: 05/01/98

Value by Tag Generation/Variation:

1st **$405-420**
2nd **$210-225**
3rd **$35-40**
4th **$13-15**
5th **$10-12**

Squirmy

Released: 6/24/00
Retired: 12/15/00

Value by Tag Generation/Variation:

6th **$5-7**
7th **$4-6**

Starlett

Released: 07/31/01
Retired: 11/08/02

Value by Tag Generation/Variation:

7th **$4-6**
9th **$4-6**
10th **$4-6**

Steg

Released: 06/03/95
Retired: 06/15/96

Value by Tag Generation/Variation:

3rd **$290-305**

Stilts

Released: 01/01/99
Retired: 05/31/99

Value by Tag Generation/Variation:

5th **$4-6**

Sting

Released: 06/03/95
Retired: 01/01/97

Value by Tag Generation/Variation:

3rd **$65-70**
4th **$38-42**

Stinger

Released: 05/30/98
Retired: 12/31/98

Value by Tag Generation/Variation:

5th **$4-6**

Stinky

Released: 06/03/95
Retired: 09/28/98

Value by Tag Generation/Variation:

3rd **$35-37**
4th **$14-16**
5th **$9-11**

Stretch

Released: 12/31/97
Retired: 03/31/99

Value by Tag Generation/Variation:

5th **$4-6**

Stripes

Released: 06/03/96
Retired: 05/01/98

Value by Tag Generation/Variation:

3rd Narrow stripes. . . **$80-85**
4th Wide stripes **$12-14**
5th Wide stripes **$9-11**

Strut

Released: 07/12/97
Retired: 03/31/99

<u>Value by Tag Generation/Variation:</u>

4th **$6-8**
5th **$6-8**

Sunny

Released: 11/28/00
Retired: 12/08/00

<u>Value by Tag Generation/Variation:</u>

6th **$7-9**

Sunray

Released: 04/30/03
Retired: n/a

Value by Tag Generation/Variation:

11th **$4-6**

Swampy

Released: 02/13/00
Retired: 03/23/01

Value by Tag Generation/Variation:

6th **$4-6**
7th **$5-7**

Swirly

Released: 05/01/99
Retired: 12/23/99

Value by Tag Generation/Variation:

5th **$4-6**

Swoop

Released: 02/13/00
Retired: 06/11/01

Value by Tag Generation/Variation:

6th **$4-6**
7th **$4-6**

Tabasco

Released: 06/03/95
Retired: 01/01/97

Value by Tag Generation/Variation:

3rd **$50-55**
4th **$38-42**

Tabs

Released: 11/27/02
Retired: n/a

Value by Tag Generation/Variation:

10th **$4-6**

Tangles

Released: 08/28/03
Retired: n/a

Value by Tag Generation/Variation:

11th **$4-6**

Tank

Released: 01/07/95
Retired: 01/07/96

Value by Tag Generation/Variation:

3rd 7 lines. **$115-125**
4th 7 lines. **$40-45**
4th 9 lines. **$150-160**
4th Shell **$58-62**

Teddy (100th Anniversary)

Released: 06/28/02
Retired: 12/27/02

Value by Tag Generation/Variation:

7th.	$5-8
10th.	$4-6

Teddy - Old Face

Released: 06/25/94
Retired: 01/07/95

Value by Tag Generation/Variation:

1st Brown	$700-715
1st Cranberry	$615-630
1st Jade	$640-655
2nd Brown	$620-635
2nd Cranberry	$1,160-1,180
2nd Jade	$680-695

Teddy - Old Face (continued)

Released: 06/25/94
Retired: 01/07/95

Value by Tag Generation/Variation:

1st Magenta	**$705-725**
1st Teal	**$675-690**
1st Violet	**$775-790**
2nd Magenta	**$590-605**
2nd Teal	**$610-630**
2nd Violet	**$715-730**

Teddy - New Face

Released: 01/07/95
Retired: 10/01/97

Value by Tag Generation/Variation:

2nd Brown	**$295-320**
2nd Cranberry	**$590-610**
2nd Jade	**$685-710**
3rd Brown	**$90-100**
3rd Cranberry	**$600-625**
3rd Jade	**$585-605**
4th Brown	**$35-50**

Teddy - New Face (continued)

Released: 01/07/95
Retired: 10/01/97

Value by Tag Generation/Variation:

2nd Magenta	**$600-620**
2nd Teal	**$605-625**
2nd Violet	**$545-565**
3rd Magenta	**$585-600**
3rd Teal	**$585-610**
3rd Violet	$585-605

TED-e

Released: 08/07/02
Retired: 08/12/02

Value by Tag Generation/Variation:

10th	**$5-7**

The Beginning

Released: 02/13/00
Retired: 05/10/00

Value by Tag Generation/Variation:

6th **$12-14**

The End

Released: 08/31/99
Retired: 01/05/00

Value by Tag Generation/Variation:

5th **$9-11**

TIGER (Zodiac)

Released: 08/19/00
Retired: 05/24/01

Value by Tag Generation/Variation:

6th. **$6-8**

Tiny

Released: 01/01/99
Retired: 01/05/00

Value by Tag Generation/Variation:

5th. **$5-7**

Tiptoe

Released: 05/01/99
Retired: 10/21/99

Value by Tag Generation/Variation:

5th **$4-6**

Toast

Released: 07/01/03
Retired: 11/25/03

Value by Tag Generation/Variation:

11th **$4-6**

Tommy

Released: 08/23/03
Retired: 12/26/03

Value by Tag Generation/Variation:

11th **$4-6**

Tooter

Released: 07/30/02
Retired: 02/28/03

Value by Tag Generation/Variation:

7th **$6-9**
10th **$5-8**

Toothy

Released: 04/01/02
Retired: 09/25/02

<u>Value by Tag Generation/Variation:</u>

5th **$5-8**
6th **$5-8**

Tracker

Released: 05/30/98
Retired: 11/26/99

<u>Value by Tag Generation/Variation:</u>

5th **$5-7**

Tracks

Released: 02/01/02
Retired: 06/25/02

Value by Tag Generation/Variation:

7th. $6-8
10th. $5-7

Tradee

Released: 06/26/01
Retired: 05/21/02

Value by Tag Generation/Variation:

6th $120-135
9th. $5-8

Trap

Released: 06/25/94
Retired: 06/15/95

Value by Tag Generation/Variation:

1st $395-415
2nd $350-360
3rd $510-525

Tricks

Released: 07/08/00
Retired: 06/18/01

Value by Tag Generation/Variation:

6th $4-7
7th $5-9

Tricky

Released: 07/31/03
Retired: 10/31/03

Value by Tag Generation/Variation:

11th. **$4-6**

Trumpet

Released: 02/13/00
Retired: 04/18/01

Value by Tag Generation/Variation:

6th. **$5-7**
7th. **$4-6**

Tubbo

Released: 04/30/03
Retired: n/a

Value by Tag Generation/Variation:

11th **$4-6**

Tuffy

Released: 05/11/97
Retired: 12/31/98

Value by Tag Generation/Variation:

4th **$5-7**
5th **$4-6**

TURK-e

Released: 11/04/02
Retired: 11/29/02

Value by Tag Generation/Variation:

10th. **$6-9**

Tusk

Released: 01/07/95
Retired: 01/01/97

Value by Tag Generation/Variation:

3rd. **$50-55**
4th. **$333-35**

Twigs

Released: 01/07/96
Retired: 05/01/98

Value by Tag Generation/Variation:

3rd **$32-36**
4th **$9-11**
5th **$9-11**

Twitterbug

Released: 12/27/02
Retired: 03/27/03

Value by Tag Generation/Variation:

7th **$6-8**
11th **$5-7**

TY 2K

Released: 08/31/99
Retired: 12/23/99

Value by Tag Generation/Variation:

5th **$7-9**

U.S.A.

Released: 06/06/00
Retired: 04/06/01

Value by Tag Generation/Variation:

6th **$6-8**

Valentina

Released: 01/01/99
Retired: 12/23/99

Value by Tag Generation/Variation:

5th $5-7

Valentino

Released: 01/07/95
Retired: 12/31/98

Value by Tag Generation/Variation:

2nd $250-275
3rd $65-70
4th $12-14
5th $7-9

Valor

Released: 09/11/03
Retired: 11/28/03

Value by Tag Generation/Variation:

11th. $4-6

Velvet

Released: 06/03/95
Retired: 10/01/97

Value by Tag Generation/Variation:

3rd $25-30
4th. $12-14

Virunga

Released: 06/01/03
Retired: 07/01/03

Value by Tag Generation/Variation:

11th **$4-6**

Waddle

Released: 06/03/95
Retired: 05/01/98

Value by Tag Generation/Variation:

3rd **$24-26**
4th **$14-16**
5th **$9-11**

Wallace

Released: 08/31/99
Retired: 12/23/99

Value by Tag Generation/Variation:

5th. **$5-7**

Waves

Released: 05/11/97
Retired: 05/01/98

Value by Tag Generation/Variation:

4th. **$5-7**

Web

Released: 06/25/94
Retired: 01/07/96

Value by Tag Generation/Variation:

1st **$535-550**
2nd. **$610-635**
3rd **$265-285**

Weenie

Released: 01/07/96
Retired: 05/01/98

Value by Tag Generation/Variation:

3rd **$30-35**
4th **$10-12**
5th **$7-11**

Whiskers

Released: 07/08/00
Retired: 04/11/01

Value by Tag Generation/Variation:

6th. **$4-6**
7th. **$4-6**

Whisper

Released: 05/30/98
Retired: 12/23/99

Value by Tag Generation/Variation:

5th. **$4-6**

White

Released: 07/01/03
Retired: 07/14/03

Value by Tag Generation/Variation:

11th $4-6

Wiggly

Released: 02/13/00
Retired: 03/27/01

Value by Tag Generation/Variation:

6th $4-6
7th $4-6

Wise

Released: 05/30/98
Retired: 12/31/98

Value by Tag Generation/Variation:

5th. **$5-7**

Wiser

Released: 05/01/99
Retired: 08/27/99

Value by Tag Generation/Variation:

5th **$4-6**

Wisest

Released: 05/01/00
Retired: 12/15/00

Value by Tag Generation/Variation:

6th $4-6
7th $5-7

Wish

Released: 03/31/03
Retired: n/a

Value by Tag Generation/Variation:

11th $4-6

Woody

Released: 08/29/02
Retired: 02/24/03

<u>Value by Tag Generation/Variation:</u>

7th. **$5-7**
10th. **$4-6**

Wrinkles

Released: 06/15/96
Retired: 09/22/98

<u>Value by Tag Generation/Variation:</u>

4th. **$5-7**
5th. **$5-7**

Yours Truly

Released: 03/21/03
Retired: 04/09/03

Value by Tag Generation/Variation:

11th **$10-12**

Zero

Released: 09/30/98
Retired: 12/31/98

Value by Tag Generation/Variation:

5th **$4-6**

Zeus

Released: 02/28/03
Retired: n/a

Value by Tag Generation/Variation:

11th. **$4-6**

Ziggy

Released: 06/03/95
Retired: 05/01/98

Value by Tag Generation/Variation:

3rd **$35-40**
4th **$10-12**
5th **$8-10**

Zip

Released: 01/07/96
Retired: 05/01/98

Value by Tag Generation/Variation:

2nd White face . . . **$485-505**
3rd All black **$180-210**
3rd White face. . . . **$195-220**
3rd White paws. **$45-50**
4th White paws. **$10-12**
5th White paws. **$6-8**

Zoom

Released: 07/30/02
Retired: n/a

Value by Tag Generation/Variation:

7th **$6-8**
10th **$7-10**

Ty Attic Treasures

Ty introduced the first twelve Attic Treasures in 1993 and produced more than 230 through 1992. Unlike Ty's other creations, Attic Treasures feature moveable joints. Possibly the most desirable Attic Treasure is the version of Tyra the cheerleader with pom poms. She was recalled shortly after her release because the pom poms were considered a choking hazard to small children. All Attic Treasures are retired, and it seems unlikely that any new ones will be created.

Alfalfa

$1-3

Allura

$2-4

Amore

$2-4

Armstrong

$2-4

Azure

$2-5

Baron

$3-6

Beargundy

$1-2

Bearkhardt

$2-4

Beezee

$2-5

Berkley

$2-4

Beverly

$3-5

Blarney

$3-5

Bluebeary

$2-4

Breezy

$3-5

Bugsy

$3-5

Calliope

$2-4

Carson

$2-4

Casanova

$1-3

Checkers

$2-6

Chelsea

$2-5

Cheri

$3-8

Cody

$3-5

Cromwell

$2-4

Darlene

$3-5

Dexter

$8-20

Easton

$1-3

Esmerelda

$2-4

Fairbanks

$1-3

Fairchild

$2-4

Franny

$2-6

Gordon

$3-5

Gwyndolyn

$2-5

Harper

$2-5

Hayes

$1-3

Ivan

$2-6

Klause

$2-5

Lawrence

$2-4

Marigold

$1-2

Merwyn

$3-5

Mulligan

$3-5

Orion

$1-3

Peppermint

$4-6

Peter

$1-3

Piccadilly

$1-4

Rafaella

$2-4

Ramsey

$1-3

Rosalie

$1-2

Salty

$1-3

Scarlet

$1-3

Skylar

$3-5

Susannah

$1-3

Tyrone

$3-6

Ty Basket Beanies

Basket Beanies are Ty's Easter series. Six were produced in spring 2002, and another four in spring 2003. At about three inches tall, Basket Beanies, like Jingle Beanies, are much smaller than Beanie Babies and have ribbon loops sewn to their tops so they can be hung as decorations. All ten Basket Beanies are retired, but Ty may produce new versions in future years.

Chickie

$1-2

Eggbert

$1-2

Eggs I

$1-2

Eggs II

$1-2

Eggs III

$1-2

Ewey

$1-2

Floppity

$1-2

Grace

$1-2

Hippie

$1-2

Hippity

$1-2

Ty Beanie Boppers

Ty introduced the first six Beanie Boppers in June 2001. These figures are modeled after children and incorporate various personalities. For example, they have interests in sports, music, and fashion. Boppers even have their own profiles listed on the Ty Web site, revealing information such as their hometowns (real cities in the United States), pets, and favorite school subjects.

Bubbly Betty

$2-4

Cuddly Crystal

$4-10

Dazzlin' Destiny

$2-5

Festive Frannie

$4-6

Glitzy Gabby

$2-4

Holiday Heidi

$8-13

Huggable Holly

$2-4

Jazzy Jessie

$3-5

Jolly Janie

$5-8

Kooky Kandy

$2-4

Loveable Lulu

$2-4

Merry Margaret

$3-5

Pretty Patti

$2-4

Rockin' Rosie

$3-5

Rugged Rusty

$2-4

Sassy Star

$5-7

Ty Beanie Buddies

Beanie Buddies entered the market in 1998 as large counterparts of Beanie Babies. But they weren't only bigger. They were also softer, sporting Ty's newly developed and patented fabric called Tylon. Each bolt of Tylon must be shipped to a number of countries to undergo various steps in its manufacture, which can take several months. The Beanie Buddy series remains one of Ty's most popular, with over forty-five versions currently available.

Ariel

$2-4

B.B. Bear

$4-6

Beak

$5-8

Billionaire

$6-8

Cheeks

$6-8

Clubby

$3-5

Employee Bear

$5-7

Erin

$2-4

Flip

$5-7

Frolic

$5-7

Fuzz

$3-6

Groovy

$5-7

Halo

$6-8

Halo II

$3-5

Hippie

$5-7

Humphrey

$3-5

Jake

$5-7

Kicks

$3-5

Libearty

$6-8

Osito

$5-7

Peace

$5-7

Peanut

$4-6

Princess

$5-7

Quackers

$5-7

Rover

$4-6

Siam

$6-8

Silver

$4-6

Spangle

$5-7

Stretch

$3-5

Sunny

$5-7

Teddy (Magenta)

$5-7

The Beginning

$8-12

Ty 2K

$5-7

Valentino

$5-7

Waddle

$2-4

Wallace

$5-7

Ty Beanie Kids

Beanie Kids made their debut in 2000 with nine versions. By the end of 2003, the only current Beanie Kid was Bab-e 2003. Beanie Kids are quite a bit larger than Beanie Babies. As their name suggests, they resemble human babies, not animals. They feature details such as sewn belly buttons and handpainted crystal eyes. Ty even offers a line of clothing to dress them.

Angel

$2-4

BABE-e

$6-8

BAB-e 2003

$3-5

Blondie

$3-5

Boomer

$1-2

Buzz

$2-4

Calypso

$3-5

Chipper

$1-3

Cookie

$2-4

Curly

$3-5

Cutie

$2-4

Dumplin'

$2-5

Ginger

$1-3

Jammer

$1-3

Luvie

$3-5

Noelle

$3-5

Precious

$2-4

Princess

$1-3

Rascal

$1-3

Shenanigan

$2-4

Specs

$3-5

Sweetie

$3-5

Tumbles

$2-4

Ty Classic

Ty introduced the Classic line in 2000, which continues to thrive with more than ninety current versions available. Three of the most unusual—Godzilla, King Ghidorah, and Mothra—are Japan exclusives issued shortly before a Japanese movie about these monsters was released in December 2001.

Al E. Kat (Orange)

$5-7

Allioop

$15-18

Baby Iceberg

$6-8

Bamboo

$5-7

Belvedere

$4-6

Glamour

$6-8

Hightops

$3-5

Lilacbeary

$2-4

Meadow

$7-9

Mercury

$6-9

Nuzzle

$4-6

Opal

$7-9

Piston

$6-8

Purplebeary

$3-5

Romeo

$2-4

Teddybearsary

$5-7

Ty Jingle Beanies

Jingle Beanies were first released in 2001 and have been perennial favorites ever since. New releases are featured in the fall for the Christmas season. Jingle Beanies are similar to Basket Beanies because they are holiday releases, they have ribbon loops for hanging, and at approximately three inches tall, they are much smaller than Beanie Babies.

1997 Hol. Teddy

$1-3

1998 Hol. Teddy

$1-3

1999 Hol. Teddy

$1-3

2000 Hol. Teddy

$1-3

2001 Hol. Teddy
$1-3

2002 Hol. Teddy
$1-3

Chillin'
$1-3

Clubby
$1-3

Clubby II

$1-3

Clubby III

$1-3

Clubby IV

$1-3

Decade

$1-3

Dizzy

$1-3

Flaky

$1-3

Halo

$1-3

Halo II

$1-3

Herald

$1-3

Jangle

$1-3

Jinglepup

$1-3

Loosy

$1-3

Mistletoe

$1-3

Quackers

$1-3

Rover

$1-3

Santa

$1-3

Snowgirl

$1-3

The Beginning

$1-3

Twigs

$1-3

Zero

$1-3

Ty Pluffies

Pluffies appeared in 2002 and apparently are the successor to the Baby Ty line, which previously replaced the Pillow Pals series. All three lines are designed for babies, featuring a larger size and more cushion than Beanie Babies, and no parts that can be chewed off to create a choking hazard. Pluffies, however, do not contain a rattle as do the earlier two lines. All eighteen Pluffies versions are current.

Bluebeary

$3-5

Catnap

$4-6

Cloud

$3-5

Corkscrew

$3-5

Dangles

$4-6

Grazer

$3-5

Grins

$3-5

Lumpy

$3-5

Melton

$3-5

Pinks

$3-5

Plopper

$3-5

Puddles

$2-4

Puppers

$4-6

Purrz

$3-5

Slumbers

$2-4

Tubby

$3-5

Whiffer

$3-5

Winks

$3-5

Ty Punkies

Seven Punkies were available in their initial release in June 2002, which coincided with the release of the Pluffies line. Pluffies' fur features very long, soft loops of thread, giving them a distinctive shaggy coat. Twenty versions of Punkies have been made, and all are current.

Dominoes

$3-5

Flipflop

$2-4

Frizzy

$2-3

Hopscotch

$3-5

Kitty

$2-4

Pipsqueak

$2-4

Polka-Dot

$2-4

Rainbow

$3-5

Shreds

$2-3

Sizzles

$3-5

Skitters

$4-6

Slim

$3-5

Snort

$3-5

Splash

$2-4

Static

$3-5

Treetop

$3-5

Trapeze

$3-5

Twizzles

$2-4

Zig-Zag

$4-6

Ty 1997 Teenie Beanie Babies

In 1997, Ty developed Teenie Beanie Babies exclusively for a McDonald's promotion. Although Ty made about ten million of each of its ten debut Teenie Beanie Baby characters, and each was supposed to last a week, many McDonald's restaurants ran out of them within several days, and in some cases, just hours. Ty and McDonald's apparently underestimated the popularity of the promotion, which is now considered the most successful in fast-food history.

Chocolate

$1-2

Chops

$1-2

Goldie

$1-2

Lizz

$1-2

Patti

$1-2

Pinky

$1-2

Quacks

$1-2

Seamore

$1-2

Snort

$1-2

Speedy

$1-2

Ty 1998 Teenie Beanie Babies

The 1997 Teenie Beanie Baby campaign was so popular that McDonald's repeated it the following year, this time offering twelve characters instead of ten and ordering approximately twenty million of each. The Teenie Beanie Baby craze further fueled the Beanie Baby mania, and prices began to sky-rocket. Adults were no longer just giving them to their children as toys; they began collecting them as investments.

Bones

$1-2

Bongo

$1-2

Doby

$1-2

Happy

$1-2

Inch

$1-2

Mel

$1-2

Peanut

$1-2

Pinchers

$1-2

Scoop

$1-2

Twigs

$1-2

Waddles

$1-2

Zip

$1-2

Ty 1999 Teenie Beanie Babies

Once again, the overwhelming success of the previous year's Teenie Beanie Baby promotion prompted McDonald's to continue its campaign, this time increasing its line to sixteen characters, and for the first time, offering four international Teenie Beanie bears—Britannia (England), Erin (Ireland), Glory (United States), and Maple (Canada).

Antsy

$1-2

Britannia

$1-2

Chip

$1-2

Claude

$1-2

Erin

$1-2

Freckles

$1-2

Glory

$1-2

Iggy

$1-2

Maple

$1-2

Nook

$1-2

Nuts

$1-2

Rocket

$1-2

Smoochy

$1-2

Spunky

$1-2

Stretchy

$1-2

Strut

$1-2

Ty 2000 Teenie Beanie Babies

The McDonald's Teenie Beanie Baby promotion culminated in its 2000 campaign. It increased the number of characters available to eighteen. The fast-food chain also offered special issue Teenie Beanie Baby boxed sets during this promotion. After this year, however, the Teenie Beanie Baby craze had run its course, and McDonald's chose not to continue it in 2001.

Blizz

$1-2

Bumble

$1-2

Bushy

$1-2

Coral

$1-2

Dotty

$1-2

Flip

$1-2

Flitter

$1-2

Goochy

$1-2

Lips

$1-2

Lucky

$1-2

Neon

$1-2

Schweetheart

$1-2

Slither

$1-2

Spike

$1-2

Spinner

$1-2

Springy

$1-2

Sting

$1-2

Tusk

$1-2

Ty 2000 Teenie Beanie Boxed Sets

In the final year of its Teenie Beanie Baby campaign, McDonald's offered several special collector's edition sets, with each character in its own plastic bubble-and-cardboard packaging. The sets available were a dinosaur trio, a U.S.A. trio, an international bear trio, a legends trio, a Ronald McDonald House Charities Millennium bear, and The End bear.

Bronty

$1-2

Chilly

$1-2

Germania

$1-2

Humphrey

$1-2

Lefty

$1-2

Libearty

$1-2

Millennium

$1-2

Osito

$1-2

Peanut

$1-2

Rex

$1-2

Righty

$1-2

Spangle

$1-2

Steg

$1-2

The End

$1-2

Ty Teenie Beanie Boppers

Teenie Beanie Boppers are a smaller version of their Beanie Bopper siblings (approximately eight inches high versus twelve inches). Like their bigger version, Teenie Beanie Boppers each have their own page on the Ty Web site displaying information about their personalities and interests.

Ace Anthony

$2-3

American Millie

$2-3

Beautiful Belle

$2-3

Brave Buddy

$3-4

Captain

$5-7

Caring Carla

$2-3

Chillin' Charlie

$2-3

Classy Cassie

$2-3

Cool Cassidy

$2-4

Cross-Court Cathy

$2-3

Darling Daisy

$2-3

Dear Debbie

$1-3

Footie

$1-3

Glitzy Gabby

$1-3

Hat-Trick Hunter

$3-5

Home Run Hank

$3-5

Jazzy Jessie

$4-6

Kool Katy

$1-3

Lucky Linda

$1-3

Midfield Mandy

$1-3

Paula Plappertasche

$2-4

Playful Peggy

$1-3

Pretty Penelope

$2-4

Private Pete

$1-3

Rockin' Ruby

$1-3

Rugged Rusty

$1-3

Sailor Sam

$1-3

Sassy Star

$2-4

Snappy Cindy

$1-3

Snazzy Sabrina

$1-3

Sunny Sue

$1-3

Sweet Sally

$1-3

Classic Collecticritters

Collecticritter bears represent various celebrities, places, or events. Each bear displays a representative embroidered symbol. For example, the Elizabeth Taylor bear displays diamonds, and the Hawaii bear features a pineapple. Each collecticritter character is produced in a sequentially numbered limited edition of ten thousand or less and includes a tag protector.

2

$1-2

Amber

$1-2

Bryant

$1-2

Chubby

$1-2

Elizabeth

$1-2

Elton

$1-2

Emerald

$1-2

Georgia

$1-2

Hawaii

$1-2

Homer

$1-2

Jack

$1-2

Jackie

$1-2

K

$1-2

Love

$1-2

Rocky

$1-2

Ruby

$1-2

Senator (Red)

$1-2

Senator (White)

$1-2

Shirley

$1-2

Sonny

$1-2

T.D.

$1-2

Topaz

$1-2

Turquoise

$1-2

Y

$1-2

Coca-Cola Bean Bag Plush

Coca-Cola bean bags are made by Cavanagh, a leading manufacturer of beanies. Major Coca-Cola beanie series include the International and Nascar series. Coca-Cola also offers miscellaneous mass market collectibles featuring some of its most recognizable cold-weather friends like the polar bear, seal, and penguin.

Coca-Cola International
Series One to Five

The fifty Coca-Cola 1999 international beanies were released in five sets of ten, each representing a country where Coca-Cola is sold. Coca-Cola also released a fifty-first beanie named Totonca the Buffalo, representing the United States, as a Coca-Cola Collector's Society Member exclusive issue. Each beanie's hang tag displays its national flag.

Ardie

$1-2

Badgey

$1-2

Baltic

$1-2

Barris

$1-2

Barrot

$1-2

Blubby

$1-2

Can Can

$1-2

Clomp

$1-2

Croon

$1-2

Crunch

$1-2

Curry

$1-2

Dover

$1-2

Fannie

$1-2

Gourmand

$1-2

Heetah

$1-2

Hopps

$1-2

Howls

$1-2

Kelp

$1-2

Key Key

$1-2

Laffs

$1-2

Lochs

$1-2

Lors

$1-2

Masa

$1-2

Masha

$1-2

Meeska

$1-2

Nardie

$1-2

Neppy

$1-2

Oppy

$1-2

Orany

$1-2

Paco

$1-2

Peng

$1-2

Pock

$1-2

Quala

$1-2

Ramel

$1-2

Reegle

$1-2

Rhiny

$1-2

Rifraff

$1-2

Rilly

$1-2

Salty

$1-2

Streak

$1-2

Strudel

$1-2

Taps

$1-2

Toolu

$1-2

Topus

$1-2

Toro

$1-2

Vaca

$1-2

Waks

$1-2

Waller

$1-2

Woolsy

$1-2

Zongshi

$1-2

Coca-Cola Nascar

Coca-Cola has been an avid sponsor of Nascar drivers for many years. To commemorate this relationship, Coca-Cola created the Nascar series, featuring America's favorite racers. Each polar bear beanie wears a shirt or jacket bearing the number and signature of a Nascar legend.

Jeff Burton	**Dale Earnhardt**
$1-2	$1-2

Dale Earnhardt

$1-2

D. Earnhardt Jr.

$1-2

D. Earnhardt Jr.

$1-2

Bill Elliot

$1-2

Kenny Irwin

$1-2

Dale Jarrett

$1-2

Bobby Labonte

$1-2

Steve Park

$1-2

Adam Petty

$1-2

Kyle Petty

$1-2

Ricky Rudd

$1-2

Tony Stewart

$1-2

Coca-Cola Miscellaneous

Coca-Cola's polar bear is one of the advertising industry's most memorable characters. The bear and his friends—the seal, penguin, reindeer, walrus, husky, and killer whale—all emphasize the ice-cold freshness of the popular soft drink. The characters wear various combinations of sweaters, scarves, hats, and uniforms to give them distinct personalities.

Bear 2000

$3-5

Bear Girl 2000

$3-5

Soda Jerk Uniform

$3-5

Checkered Ball Cap

$3-5

Red Scarf/Ball Cap

$3-5

Yellow Ball Cap

$3-5

Blue Snowflake Hat

$3-5

Green Scarf/Ski Hat

$3-5

Snowflake Hat

$3-5

Red Coca-Cola Hat

$3-5

Coca-Cola Scarf

$3-5

Green/Red Shirt

$3-5

Blue Shirt

$3-5

Red Scarf/Shirt

$3-5

Baseball Uniform

$3-5

Golf Shirt

$3-5

Skier

$3-5

Football Jersey

$3-5

Fireman

$3-5

Policeman

$3-5

Husky

$3-5

Jaguar

$3-5

Killer Whale

$3-5

2000 Penguin

$3-5

Grn. Hat/Striped Vest

$3-5

Red Coca-Cola Scarf

$3-5

Green Vest

$3-5

Pilot Goggles/Scarf

$3-5

Hockey Shirt

$3-5

Chef

$3-5

Reindeer

$3-5

Red Scarf

$3-5

Red Coca Cola Hat

$3-5

Checkered Hat/Vest

$3-5

2000 Seal

$3-5

Red Hat/Scarf

$3-5

Long Green Scarf

$3-5

Starry Scarf

$3-5

Green Bowtie/Vest

$3-5

Baseball Cap

$3-5

Striped Cap/Blue Vest

$3-5

Chef

$3-5

Soccer Uniform

$3-5

Walrus

$3-5

Red Coca-Cola Hat

$3-5

Coca-Cola Scarf

$3-5

Disney Mini Bean Bag Plush

With its enormous number of animated characters, its worldwide influence, and a huge following of dedicated collectors, Disney is a natural match for beanies. Disney has produced beanies of characters from classic movies like *Winnie-the-Pooh* and *Pinocchio*, as well as newer releases like *Mulan*. Disney beanies carry a wide variety of hang tags from its Club Disney, Disney store, theme parks, and international series.

Bashful

$5-7

Chip

$3-5

Cri-Kee

$3-5

Cruella DeVille

$5-7

Daisy Duck

$6-8

Doug

$3-5

Eeyore

$6-8

Fairfolk

$3-5

Genie

$5-7

Hen Wen

$3-5

Jiminy Cricket

$5-7

Lil' Brother

$3-5

Mickey Mouse

$6-8

Mickey Astronaut

$6-8

Minnie Santa

$6-8

Mushu

$3-5

Piglet

$6-8

Pinocchio

$5-7

Tigger

$6-8

Timon

$5-7

Winnie the Pooh

$6-8

Winnie/Sweater

$6-8

Winnie Snowman

$6-8

Winnie Santa

$6-8

Grateful Dead Bean Bears

Grateful Dead Beanie Bears are based on characters from Grateful Dead songs and are manufactured by Liquid Blue. All beanies use a single body style but feature a wide variety of wild colors and designs. The beanies display tags hung around their necks rather than traditional hang tags fastened by a plastic attachment. Each tag lists the beanie's name, birthdate, and an anecdote from a tour.

Ashbury

$6-9

Black Peter

$15-20

Candyman

$5-8

Cosmic Charlie

$6-9

Crazy Fingers

$6-9

Daisy

$9-12

Dark Star

$9-12

Daydream

$6-9

Deal

$9-12

Dupree

$6-9

Fall Tour

$9-12

Father Time

$6-9

Fire

$9-12

Franklin

$4-7

Irie

$6-9

Jack A Roe

$6-9

Jerry

$4-6

Lost Sailor

$6-9

Peggy-O

$6-9

Ripple

$6-9

Scarlet

$9-12

Snowflake

$6-9

Sunshine

$6-9

Terrapin

$3-5

Harley-Davidson Bean Bag Plush

Harley-Davidson Beanies are manufactured by Cavanagh, the same company that makes Coca-Cola beanies. The most common Harley-Davidson beanie characters are bears, bulldogs, and pigs. Others include sheep, frogs, bulls, cows, raccoons, skunks, and walruses. Each is equipped with riding accessories like boots, jacket, helmet, hat, bandanna, or goggles.

Big Twin

$3-5

Boot Hill Bob

$3-5

Bravo

$3-5

Bubba

$3-5

Clutch Carbo

$3-5

Fat Bob

$3-5

Kickstart

$3-5

Manifold Max

$3-5

Motorhead Bob

$3-5

Punky

$3-5

Ratchet

$3-5

Revit

$3-5

Roamer

$3-5

Spotts

$3-5

Starke

$3-5

Stroker

$3-5

Tanker

$3-5

Thunder

$3-5

Torque

$3-5

Tusk

$3-5

Meanies

The name "Meanies" is a parody of the generic term "beanies." As their name suggests, Meanies are a coarse version of their gentler, more innocent cousins. Some Meanies are caricatures of celebrities—Quack Nicholson (Jack Nicholson), for example. Others lampoon traditional icons like Slushy the Snowman (Frosty the Snowman), while still others incorporate animals in a play on words, such as Bad Hare Day.

Armydillo Dan

$2-3

Boris the Mucosaurus

$2-3

Burny the Bear

$2-3

Chicken Pox

$2-3

The Cod Father

$2-3

Cold Turkey

$2-3

Dennis Rodmantis

$2-3

Donkeyng

$2-3

Fangaroo

$2-3

Fi & Do the Dalmutation

$2-3

Floaty the Fish

$2-3

Jerry Stinger

$2-3

Lucky the Rabbit

$2-3

Matt the Fat Bat

$2-3

Mick Jaguar

$2-3

Mike Bison

$2-3

Moodonna

$2-3

Navy Seal

$2-3

Phlemingo

$2-3

Quack Nicholson

$2-3

**Slushy the
Snowman**

$2-3

Snake Eyes Jake

$2-3

**Splat the Road Kill
Cat**

$2-3

**Sunny the Preemie
Chickie**

$2-3

Peaceables

Peaceable Planet, the manufacturer of the Peaceables line of beanies, has produced two series of country and state beanies, with each beanie bearing a flag. The company limits production to 72,000 of each animal and donates part of its profits to organizations that promote world peace. It also has produced a special edition set of three monkeys called Clarity, Harmony, and Frank to promote the principle, "hear no evil, see no evil, speak no evil."

Aloha

$1-2

Hue (Mickey) Manatee

$1-2

Ludwig

$1-2

Maximus

$1-2

Myrtle

$1-2

Sherbet O'Shear

$1-2

Uncle Sammy

$1-2

Winston

$1-2

Puffkins

Puffkins are brightly colored, square-shaped beanies created by Swibco, a manufacturer of souvenir and novelty items. Like Ty, Swibco provides an interactive beanie site, where parents and children can read newsletters, enter comments on a discussion board, or play games. The site does not accept orders, however. Purchases must be made through retailers.

Buttercup

$2-3

Casey

$2-3

Cosmo

$2-3

Dillard

$2-3

Fetch

$2-3

Gertie

$2-3

Gus

$2-3

Henrietta

$2-3

Honey

$2-3

Jack

$2-3

Jake

$2-3

Jules

$2-3

Mango

$2-3

Mystic

$22-24

Omar

$2-3

Patches

$2-3

Rosie

$2-3

Shadow

$2-3

Skylar

$2-3

Spice

$2-3

Squawk

$2-3

Stitch

$2-3

Strut

$2-3

Swoop

$2-3

Salvino's Bammers

Salvino's Bammers are primarily sports-related beanies emphasizing baseball, but beanies featuring football, hockey, and other sports are offered as well. On team-sport beanies, the name and number of the celebrity athlete is embroidered on the beanie. Bammers were so popular at one point that the company expanded its line to include entertainers such as country music artists like Alan Jackson and Faith Hill.

John Elway

$3-5

Wayne Gretzky

$3-5

Ken Griffey Jr.

$3-5

Dave Justice/Holiday

$3-5

**McGwire/
Collector's Club**

$3-5

**McGwire/
Commemorative**

$3-5

**McGwire/
Home Run Kings**

$3-5

McGwire/Promo

$3-5

Jake Plummer

$3-5

Nolan Ryan

$3-5

Save the Children Bean Bag Plush

The Save the Children Foundation introduced this beanie line to raise funds for its ongoing effort to improve the living conditions for children around the world. A portion of the retail price is used to help the foundation offset costs of sponsoring children and funding food, medical, and educational programs. The beanies feature children from various cultures and countries and are dressed in colorful clothing.

Damita

$1-2

Erik

$1-2

Haruko

$1-2

Juji

$1-2

Jun

$1-2

Kachina

$1-2

MacKenzie

$1-2

Patrick

$1-2

Paz

$1-2

Sila

$1-2

Stella

$1-2

Stephane

$1-2

Warner Brothers
Studio Store Bean Bags

Like Disney, Warner Brothers has a large pool of animated movie and television characters from which to make beanies. And like its counterpart Disney beanies, Warner Brothers beanies come with a wide variety of hang tags, such as holiday, movie, talking beanie, and Cartoon Network editions. Scooby-Doo and the Tasmanian Devil are favorites and have been produced in countless versions.

Huckleberry

$1-2

Petunia

$1-2

Scooby

$5-7

Scooby/N.Y.

$5-7

Tasmanian Devil

$4-6

Tweety

$4-6

Glossary

TERMS:

Current: A bean bag still being produced and available for sale from the manufacturer and/or authorized dealers.

Discontinued: A bean bag no longer being manufactured but not yet officially retired.

Exclusive: A bean bag that is distributed only for a particular country or event.

Generation: The style of hang tag or tush tag attached to a beanie. Tag generations are numbered in succession—first generation, second generation, etc.

Hang Tag: The cardboard tag attached to a beanie. It is sometimes called a swing tag because it swings loosely from its fastener.

Limited Edition: A bean bag that isn't necessarily produced for a particular area or event but is manufactured in much lower quantities than other releases of its kind.

Retired: A bean bag no longer made and whose manufacturer has officially announced that it is out of production.

Swing Tag: (see Hang Tag).

Tag Protector: A clear plastic device that slides or folds over a hang tag to keep it clean and to prevent damage.

Tush Tag: The cloth tag containing manufacturing information that is sewn into a beanie's seam.

Variation: A bean bag that a manufacturer has intentionally changed. Manufacturers most commonly modify a beanie's color.

ABBREVIATIONS:

1G, 2G, 3G, etc.: first generation tag, etc.
BB: Beanie Baby
BIN: buy it now
CDN: Canadian
CC: credit card
DL: Disneyland
DS: Disney Store
EX: excellent condition
G: good condition
G/A: guaranteed authentic
HTF: hard to find
LE: limited edition
MBBP: mini bean bag plush

MIB: mint in bag (refers to Teenie Beanie Babies in original packaging)

MIP: mint in package (refers to Teenie Beanie Babies in original packaging)

MQ: museum quality

MT: mint condition

MWBT: mint with bent tag

MWBMT: mint with both mint tags

MWMT: mint with mint tags

MWNT: mint with no tags

MWCHT: mint with creased hang tag

MWHT: mint with hang tag

MWT: mint with tag

NM: near mint condition

NR: no reserve

PP: PayPal

S/H: shipping and handling

TBB: Teenie Beanie Baby

VG: very good condition

VHTF: very hard to find

WB: Warner Brothers

WDW: Walt Disney World